LIVERPOOL
ODDITIES

RICHARD WHITTINGTON-EGAN

THE GALLERY PRESS
LEIGHTON BANASTRE, PARKGATE, SOUTH WIRRAL

ISBN 0 900389 25 7
Published by Gallery Press 1986   Reprinted 1989
© Richard Whittington-Egan
Printed by Scotprint (North West) Limited.

The Liverpool Dossier Series
All titles in this series were originally published
in Richard Whittington-Egan's earlier books
LIVERPOOL COLONNADE and LIVERPOOL
ROUNDABOUT.

Now available:—

Back in the days when the Beatles would still pop into Ye Cracke in Rice Street to take a friendly ale with me, I was paying a young man's court to the fickle jade of the Mersey. I wrote two love chronicles of our on-off affair—*Liverpool Colonnade* and *Liverpool Roundabout.* Oh, I was a knight-errant then, pricking in fancy my milk-white palfrey through the stone forest and down the avenues of my imagination. And such imaginings! I saw the Liver birds take wing against a low-lying hunter's moon . . . the chimney-masted tangle of sky-riding roof-tops looking at dusk like the decks of ships at swaying anchor . . . I heard the golden and porcelained names on windows singing the old crafts' songs and lullabies of trade . . . I lurked around the Western bazaar counters in the lit grottoes of the shops . . . I rode the overhead railway and the Noah's Ark tramcars . . . watched the glittering city slip over the horizon's edge into the purple pomp of night—and out again into the watered-milk light of another dawn. Both I and the Liverpool of which I wrote have grown up, grown different. We have played weather-vanes to the wind of change. And yet we are still the same at heart. The fresh wind blowing across the river and over my city's wild hilltop still whispers the old tales to those who are willing to listen . . . a light still burns in Paradise Street . . .

CONTENTS

1. THE LAST TIME I MET TCHAIKOVSKY

The last time I met Tchaikovsky we quarrelled—at least he quarrelled with me. Picking up his battered violin case and flinging it down again on the floor of Central Station café to emphasise his disgust, he brushed the crumbs from his somewhat off-white beard and said, "None of you ignorant Liverpool people appreciate music." I tried to protest. It was no use at all. "Two measly shillings in three hours," he muttered angrily and swept out to begin his second recital.

Tchaikovsky, I had better explain, was only his nickname. I never knew his real name for it did not appear on any bill-boards. He *was* a Russian and music *was* his profession, but his platform was the street corner. An old, bent man, grime-grained, in a tattered raincoat, he was one of that fast-disappearing band of troubadours who have, across the years, enlivened the Liverpool street scene with their alfresco entertainments. Now he has gone, exchanged his asthmatic old violin for, one hopes, a more tuneful harp, and his only memorial is a great silence in the grey streets where once he sent the notes chasing one another in plaintive pursuit of a few pennies. He has gone to join the other shades whose memories haunt our kerb-sides—shades like that of 'Harpo,' the little sharp-faced man in the pancake-flat cap who carried a zither before him as delicately as if it were a tray of crown Derby; and the old man with the mammoth white moustache who, with a concertina in his hands, drumsticks on his elbows, a huge drum on his back, a pair of cymbals attached to his heel by a string, a triangle, and a mouth-organ, held by means of a sort of iron collar to his lips, was Liverpool's only one-man band.

I doubt if in all Liverpool you could find more than half a dozen street entertainers to-day. Three of the real old-timers are still going strong. 65-year-old Harry Walker, who plays the banjo to the cinema queues and who will proudly tell you that he once did a broadcast, and Alf Morton and his partner, George, who form a musical ensemble of two with guitar and accordion. More recent recruits are one-legged Charlie 'Leggy' Norton, who strums a banjo and at the same time coaxes a tune out of a mouth-organ, and William George McMahon, a regular Saturday evening performer at Jimmy Quinn's White Star Hotel, who has these last twenty years been 'working the pubs' with his accordion.

★　★　★　★

How bare the streets seem to-day when one remembers the rich past: the ballad-singers, the barrel-organs with swarthy Italians turning the handles as monkeys in little red fezzes and jackets collected the coppers;

7

the travelling bears which danced, or rather swayed, at the ends of their chains to the wheezings of a concertina; colourful characters like the cannon-ball man who would throw a heavy cannon-ball up, catch it on his back and roll it dexterously around his shoulders and arms, and the negro whose usual pitch was a piece of waste land near Langton Dock — though sometimes he would appear at the top of James Street — who used to fling a coconut or turnip high into the air and allow it to fall and shatter itself on his forehead. Near Paddy's Market was the dancing-nigger man, an old negro who manipulated a wired frame on a trestle in front of him. Attached to the wires were numbers of little rag-dolls which danced up and down as he kept up a continuous chanting of "We have butter-milk all the week and whisky on a Sunday," and hammered an accompaniment on the frame with his knuckles. And outside Reynolds's Waxworks in Lime Street, you would as often as not hear the woeful wailing of the blind Irish piper.

There must be many who still remember 'Old Jakes,' a fine old chap who, with his long grey beard and a mane of hair that hung down to his shoulders, looked like a biblical prophet. Summer and winter he wore a heavy greatcoat which reached to his ankles, and his toes were clearly visible poking out of the ends of his boots. Between about 1910 and 1920 you could see him any day in the streets around the Cotton Exchange. His instrument was the harp, but it was such a harp as no one had ever played (including 'Old Jakes') for the strings were literally pieces of string, many of which had large knots in them. Naturally, the harp emitted no sound whatsoever, but 'Old Jakes' did his best to supply the deficiency by crooning some weird tune of his own as his fingers plucked at the unresponsive strings. The wags christened him 'The Lost Chord.'

Not far away, in Pownall Square, you could find a character known as 'Hifer Stifer.' 'Hifer' was a singer in the old ballad tradition, but his repertoire was somewhat limited. To be honest, it consisted of the chorus of one song:

> *Hi! for it. Hi! for it.*
> *Hi! for it still.*
> *Hi! for the little house*
> *— under the hill.*

This, sung over and over again, rapidly, to the accompaniment of some bells which he rattled on his wrists. How he came by the name of 'Hifer' is painfully obvious.

★　★　★　★

Characters all, these artists of the pavements were the lineal descendants of the strolling players, wandering minstrels and troubadours who from the earliest times travelled about England. They may have been ragged, often unwashed, but they must occupy a proud place in our folklore, and there is a certain rough justice in the fact that after all the long years of neglect and slowly-falling pennies their colourful wraiths should be summoned back to the drab stage of the Liverpool streets to take a tardy curtain-call.

2. PUTTING A BRAVE FACE ON IT

Somehow I can't shake off the feeling that if anyone were to ask me the name of my club and I had to reply "The Ugly Face Club," even the blandishments of those friends who would compliment me upon the nicety of my choice, and the sympathy of those enemies who regretted it, would not propitiate a certain embarrassment which the admission would cause me.

And yet, strange to relate, there did once exist in this city of surprises a club which rejoiced in just that title, and I have before me as I write a copy of the membership register upon which are inscribed the names of 55 brave Liverpool gentlemen who unhesitatingly acknowledged their physical qualifications for entry upon the roll of such a society.

★ ★ ★ ★

Ye Ugly Face Clubb of Leverpoole, or to give it its full and proper style, 'Ye Most Honourable and Facetious Society of Ugly Faces,' was formed on January 15th, 1743, and seems to have continued in existence for eleven years, until January 21st, 1754.

Its members appear to have been drawn chiefly from the merchant class—the ugly faces of commerce!—though one distorted doctor of divinity, three or four mean-visaged medicos, several squint-eyed ships' captains and a sprinkling of toad-faced tradesmen were included in its ill-formed body.

The primary condition for membership was that the aspiring candidate should exhibit "something odd, remarkable, Drol or out of the way in his Phiz, as in the length, breadth, narrowness, or in his complexion, the cast of his eyes, or make of his mouth, lips, chin, &c." The fortunate possessor of such features as a deathbed complexion, a hedgehog forehead, squinting, pig eyes, a "monstrous long nose resembling a speaking trumpet" or one "rising in the middle like a camel's hunch," a fluke mouth with "irregular bad set teeth like those of an old worn-out comb thoroughly begrim'd and a tongue like an anchovy, or a "prodigeous long chin meeting his nose like a pair of nutcrackers," was always sure of sympathetic consideration. His suitability for membership was judged of by the majority of the Society, the President having the casting vote.

★ ★ ★ ★

How well some of the members merited election is apparent from the descriptions of them which have been left for the envy of posterity.

Captain Nicholas Southworth. A fine yellow guinea complexion.

10

Large nostrils. Negro nosed. Hollow forehead. Long pucking chin. In ye whole resembles Tom Thumb in a puppet show.

Robert Moss, Esq., Councellor at Law. A long tawny visage. Lanthorn jawed. Hollow pig eyes. Large nose. A prodigious wide mouth, especially when he laughs, and looks like a Grubb Street Poett half starv'd.

Mr. Jno. Wood. July 22, 1751, of Liverpool, Architect. A stone coloured complexion. A dimple in his attic storey. The pillasters of his face fluted. Tortoise eyed. A prominent nose, wild grin and face altogether resembling a badger, and finer though smaller than Sir Christopher Wren or Inigo Jones's.

Thos. Wycliffe, Merchant in Liverpool, 22 Jany., 1753. A ghostlike complexion. Goggle eyed. A fine shrivelled face. A marl pit in his chin. Furrows in his cheeks. Bushy eye-brows. On the whole picture of a hard winter with a ghastly grin.

Henry Spendilow. A rugged face. A large, flattish nose. A fluke mouth. Thick lips. Lank jaws. Long chin. In short a charming member in every respect.

James Ashton, D.D., Chaplain to ye Society. A fine carved face. Eyelashes like two besoms. Nose like a shuffle nosed shark. Blubber lips. Meagre cheeks. A triangular mouth. Eyes of a sea green. Exceedingly well qualified member.

The President, Jos. Farmer, merchant, was, as befitted his office, unbelievably hideous—"Little Eyes one bigger than y'other. Long Nose. Thin Lanthorn Jaws. Bare upper Lip. Mouth from Ear to Ear resembling a shark's. Rotten Sett of Irregular Teeth which are sett off to great Advantage by frequent laughing. His Visage long and narrow. His looks upon the whole extraordinary, Haggard, Odd, Comick, and out of y' way. In short, possessed of every Extraordinary Qualifications to rend him y' Phoenix of y' Society, as the Like won't appear again this 1000 years."

Far from being offended by this frank assessment of his personal charms, Mr. Farmer, on being asked to accept office, wrote:

"I return you my *Hearty Thanks* for being Chosen *President* of ye Most Ancient, Numerous and Honourable Fraternity of Ugly-Faces; to which have belonged the greatest Heroes, Statesmen, Poets, Saints and Philosophers; as Homer, Alexander, Aesop, Socrates, St. Paul, Cromwell, etc., who were all as eminently remarkable for their Ugly Grotesk Phizzes as for their several Great Abilities and Extensive Knowledge."

★   ★   ★   ★

Our information concerning the Club's proceedings is unfortunately

11

very scant. Indeed, had it not been for the wind of chance which, sometimes in the late 'eighties of the last century, blew a curious old manuscript volume into the hands of Mr. Edward Howell, a Liverpool bookseller, it is doubtful if we should ever have heard of the Club at all.

The motto of the Society was *"Taetrum ante omnia vultum,"* which may be rendered, "Before all things, an ugly face," and the members met once a fortnight at the Exchange Coffee House and dined together every three months.

The rules stipulated that every person upon his being initiated into the Society should drink a bumper to the success thereof, and that "ale shall be the common drink."

The income of the Society was mainly derived from 'forfeitures' or fines, and occasional collections. Expenditure was not high, on average somewhere about £15 a year, and that was chiefly spent on eating and drinking. There are, however, one or two intriguing items such as, "By paid the barber a year's attendance, 6s.," "To cash paid the servant for Dressing a Pigg" (not a member this, one trusts!), and, most fascinating of all, "By Miss Betty Wrigley a tickett, 2s."

The members were, not surprisingly, all bachelors, and Rule Number 11 laid down "That when any member Marries he shall forfeit ten shillings and sixpence for the use of this Society." That a number of such half-guineas were in the course of time duly received only goes to show that then, as now, love was blind, beauty only skin deep and residing in the eye of the beholder.

3. TREASURE, TRAGEDY AND TRIVIA IN STORE

In these last days I have been lifting the dust-sheets that shroud a thousand dreams which crowd the chill acres of Liverpool's huge furniture storehouses.

Perhaps at a first glance such places look, with their vast tangled forests of furniture, rather like gigantic auction-rooms, but there is a subtle difference in atmosphere, for whereas the sale-room represents the end of a dream, the depository usually signifies only a temporary eclipse.

Usually, but not always.

Back in 1878 a young Liverpool girl got married. Prior to the wedding the couple had furnished a cosy little home for themselves, but tragedy struck before they were able to move into it. The husband died on his honeymoon. The grief-stricken wife immediately telegraphed to a Liverpool depository: "I cannot bear to look upon our furniture. It holds too many memories for me. Please take it away and store it." Nor did she ever see it again. For fifty years it lay, a ghostly pyramid, in the warehouse, until at last the bride, by then an old and withered woman, died, and it was sold.

"Is this a record?" I was tempted to ask. Not quite. That marathon storage was just beaten by a young medical student who, in 1900, deposited a trunk of medical books in a Liverpool warehouse. For more than half a century that trunk has never been opened, but every year the storage fee has been duly paid, and in 1955 a bent old man of seventy-seven called to pay the dues on his now valueless books.

And that is the amazing thing about the storage business. A good fifty per cent. of the objects which are stored are of little or no intrinsic worth. They are to be evaluated only in terms of sentiment. "Now take the case of the old lady who brought along two large cases which she said held her most prized possessions," said the warehouseman. "They proved to contain a large assortment of her childhood dolls, and twice a year, regular as clockwork, she would come to the warehouse and spend a couple of hours playing with them! It was really uncanny to see the slight, child-like figure with the wrinkled face kneeling there in the twilight crooning over those mouldering dolls." Shades of Miss Havisham!

Almost every depository has its trunks of faded love-letters, but one warehouseman told me of an extraordinary chest, left there twenty-four years ago by an elderly gentleman, in which are neat piles of centuries-old silk, satin, brocade, lace and frill worn by one of his ancestors.

Possibly one of the most curious objects at present lodged in any Liverpool warehouse is a spear. This spear belongs to a gentleman who lives

13

abroad, and once in the long-ago that very spear was thrown at him. A native servant pulled it out and, fortunately, the aforesaid gentleman suffered no injury more permanent than a hole in his back which, he claims, fits exactly the head of the spear. Every two years he comes on holiday to England and the depository always receives a postcard saying: "Please get my goods out." Shortly afterwards he himself arrives, the spear (which he always insists must be kept carefully wrapped up—"It is tipped with deadly poison") is produced, he gazes at it for a few minutes and that is that for another couple of years.

Another regular visitor is a man who first put in an appearance a number of years ago. He came upon the scene wearing a heavy fur overcoat, and brought with him a single large trunk which he said contained his summer clothes. The following spring he reappeared, asked for his trunk and requested permission to change his clothes. He did so and deposited his fur coat and woolly winter underwear in the trunk. And every spring and autumn since, this curious man has called to change his clothes.

From time to time among the sober piles of furniture, the rolls of carpet, the wardrobes, the dining-room suites, the broken-down mangles and the curiously pathetic little heaps of children's toys, you will find some very strange objects. The cask containing Uncle Alfred; a captain's uniform which saw service in the Crimean War; a penny-farthing bicycle; a skeleton in a black, coffin-like box from a doctor's home; bulky packages of Russian bank-notes (now worthless) stored by a fleeing Russian aristocrat at the time of the revolution; African idols; stuffed pets; the grinning head of an Egyptian mummy which was said to have come out of Pharaoh's tomb. This latter, by the way, was left unclaimed for many years and eventually the proprietor took it to his own home, but his wife said that she would not sleep with the thing in the house and it finished up as a somewhat macabre exhibit in a prominent Liverpool dentist's surgery. Once, an entire farm—excluding livestock—was put into storage and, many years ago, an old Liverpool depository stored all the animals in the menagerie of Hengler's Circus. "Feeding the lions," I was told, "was quite a problem."

But the strangest story of all is that of the day when a bronzed colonial drove up in a taxi, to the front of which was lashed a huge barrel. "Say, can I store this barrel for two or three months with you?" he asked. The manager eyed the sinister-looking barrel somewhat uneasily. "I must ask you what it contains" he said. "Opals," was the reply. And sure enough that barrel was crammed with thousands of pounds worth of precious stones. Too large to go through the door of the strong-room, the barrel was hidden beneath a pile of rubbish in the yard at the back of the depository. And there it remained until, three months later, the owner turned up with another taxi to remove his precious barrel and a great weight from the mind of the warehouseman!

4. STALKING THE LIVER BIRD

Having just spent a breathless June day in hopeless quest of the fabulous Liver Bird I am able to state categorically that ornithological invention is not the prerogative of Carroll, Lear and Araby. Jubjub, Tropical Turnspit and Roc are no more and no less nonsuch, never-were birds than Herodotus's Phoenix and Liverpool's Liver.

I speak with authority for, seizing my runcible hat and slinging a pair of powerful bird-watching binoculars across my shoulders, I have hied me to the concrete forests of the streets and searched high and low for the elusive Liver.

In the course of my hunt I found carvings and pictures of the Liver Bird in abundance; on the green belly of the bus that bore me townwards; on the facades of sundry buildings and on the paper and furniture of municipal officialdom; but it was in the quiet groves of the Picton that I discovered the first feathers as it were of the Liver.

But alas! Grim discovery. Those feathers belonged to an eagle—the eagle of St. John—and as I turned sheaf after sheaf of musty papers it became more and more painfully obvious that the Liver Bird was a myth, hatched, centuries ago, out of an eagle's egg.

It was in the year 1207 that King John, desiring a port from which to embark military supplies to Ireland, granted letters patent to Liverpool, and, twenty-two years later, his son, Henry III, gave Liverpool a charter constituting it a free borough. Anxious to celebrate its new-found freedom, the town promptly decided to adopt a corporate seal, and it may be that the eagle of St. John was chosen in judicious compliment to the House of King John—a supposition to which substance is lent by the fact that the eagle held in its beak a sprig of the Plantagenet emblem, the *planta genista* (broom pods and leaves). The seal would be made of either silver or brass—most likely silver—and only one good wax impression of it survives. It is in the muniment room at Croxteth Hall.

Liverpool lost this first seal during the siege of 1644 when Prince Rupert's troops sacked the town and carried off its plate. It was, however, replaced in 1655 by a second seal of silver (which is still in use) engraved with a bird which, because of inferior workmanship, bore not the slightest resemblance to the Evangelist's eagle. Indeed, as the centuries wore on, this somewhat nondescript bird came to be regarded as a hen cormorant which, considering the large numbers of cormorants which disport themselves in the Mersey, is scarcely surprising.

Perhaps it is not quite fair to lay all the blame for the disappearance of the eagle at the door of the unskilful engraver, for as far back as 1611 the town records were speaking of the Liverpool bird as a cormorant. The first authentic allusion to anything approaching a Liver Bird occurs in 1668 when the then Earl of Derby presented the municipality with a mace engraved with "a leaver." By April 25th, 1743, the old seal, stolen practically a century before by Prince Rupert, had been recovered by the Corporation, and on that date an order was made that the *new* seal should be destroyed.

Due to some unfortunate mistake, however, it was the old seal that was destroyed, on October 14th, 1743, and consequently the *new* seal continues in use to this day.

In 1796 a horrified town-council suddenly discovered that Liverpool in fact no ratified arms, and representations were hastily made to the College of Arms. One Alderman Clayton Tarleton was empowered to negotiate on behalf of the Corporation, and he suggested to the College that the proper bird to adorn Liverpool's crest was a "Lever or Sea Cormorant." The Heralds decided, however, that it should be a plain cormorant and specified that it should hold a branch of laver in its bill. That the bird on the old seal was intended for an eagle—the eagle of St. John—is made abundantly clear by the inscription, "Johannis,"which appears below it. Indeed, when arms were granted to the Bishopric of Liverpool in 1882 the bird was properly shown as an eagle. Thus, we have to-day the curious situation of the arms of the bishopric correctly bearing an eagle, while the arms of the Corporation are erroneously emblazoned with an ornithologically suspect cormorant.

After digesting all this I never expected to find a stuffed Liver Bird in Liverpool. But I did. It was in the basement cloak-room of the Town hall. "Once upon a time," I was told, "it stood in its glass case at the foot of the stairs, but a former Lord Mayor who has no taste for such things ordered its removal and it was hurriedly stowed away downstairs." I took with me a friend learned in ornithology. He glanced at it and pronounced: "It is a young cormorant." Rumour has it that this is the actual specimen which, in 1796, was despatched to the College of Arms to show them exactly what a "Lever or Sea Cormorant" looked like. My friend, an expert in such matters, said that of course it was *possible,* but we decided that it was far more likely that some nineteenth-century, know-all alderman had said to his Lord Mayor: "I tell you there *was* such a bird as the Liver Bird, and what is more I have one and will bring it to show you." We pictured the scene. One day the bird, carefully stuffed, was lugged along to the Town hall. The city fathers stood around in wonderment. "Well it certainly *looks* like the Liver Bird," ventured one a trifle more naive than the rest. "I tell you it *is* the Liver Bird"—this, somewhat exasperatedly, from its owner.

"Well, well, I never thought I'd live to see a stuffed Liver Bird," the Lord Mayor would say shaking his head. "It'd be all right to have it in the mayor's parlour," someone would rashly suggest. That was all that was needed. Its triumphant owner was delighted to make the gesture and Liverpool was duly given the bird.

Leaving the cormorant in the cellar, I made my way to the Liver Building and climbed 483 steps to the veritable eyrie of the Liver Bird. Three hundred odd feet up I came out from a tunnel of brick onto the windswept roof of Liverpool, and above me I saw the two 18-foot Liver Birds. There they stood, glinting green in the sunlight, their wings raised as though alerted for flight. Standing in that lonely place I had the feeling that at any moment they might wing their way off, out across the estuary to the Never-Never Land from which they came. But, happily, they moved not a metal feather, for have the wiseacres not said that the day the Liver Birds fly away, that day will see the end of Liverpool?

5. HOW TO MAKE THE PARTY GO WITH A BANG

Is November too early to start thinking of Christmas parties? Not a bit. Haven't the shops been planning their 'seasonable gifts' since June, and didn't I spot the first Christmas card in September? Anyway, since anticipation is widely held to be superior to realization, why shouldn't I savour the party spirit a month or so before the event?

As a matter of fact I have done considerably more than *think* about it; for several days now I have been making the most active preparations, and when the distinguished company of my wife's relatives descend upon us they will find everything ready for their reception.

When Great-Uncle William comes puffing in and hangs his coat up in the hall it will promptly fall to the ground—because I shall have provided a rubber coat-hook for his use. When Aunt Elspeth returns from washing her hands she is certain to give me some black looks—because I shall have put a shilling tablet of sooty-face soap in the bathroom. And there is going to be a severe shock awaiting anyone who commandeers my favourite armchair, for beneath its velvet cushion will be concealed a 'realistic cat-miaow squeaker.' If all goes according to plan, Uncle Peregrine will be cut short in his usual interminable narration concerning army life in India, because, specially for him, I have acquired an exploding cigar. Should the merriment flag, I have in reserve a number of other little surprises: a fearful, furry, black, springing thing called a Bogey-Bogey that should settle once and for all my formidable Aunt Lucretia, who is forever boasting that she is not afraid of mice: a neat contraption that fits under a plate of sandwiches and goes off with an ear-splitting report when you lift the plate, and a huge mechanical moth which I am going to secrete in a wallet which is my Christmas gift to the aforesaid Great-Uncle William. There is a certain sly symbolism about this latter, for Great-Uncle William is of a turn of nature that is politely described as careful. I did toy with the idea of presenting him with a small leather purse that traps your fingers in steel jaws when you open it but on reflection I decided that he might never discover the joke!

All these merry pranks represent the merest fraction of the hilarious stock-in-trade of a certain practical jokers' paradise in Liverpool where, in exchange for a few mundane shillings, you will be provided with 'Jokes and novelties for every occasion.' They may not help you to make friends, but you will certainly influence people.

★ ★ ★ ★

"Good afternoon," said Mr. Wilf Bennett, the manager of the Wizard's Den, crushing what appeared to be a lighted cigarette into my palm. I let out an undignified howl before discovering that it was a fake. I determined

19

to be on my guard against this joker. An attempt to catch me with a plastic cockroach, which he picked off my collar, failed, and just as I was congratulating myself on my alertness the pencil with which I was about to scribble a few notes doubled up in my hand. His assistant, Roy Pilkington, had exchanged mine for a rubber one.

"Here, use my pen," said Mr. Bennett. Like a fool, I took it. The thing exploded and splashed an ocean of ink onto my shirt-front. I went purple. "Don't worry, it's special fading ink," beamed Mr. Pilkington as he opened a sweet tin and shot three serpents at me.

Looking at all the 'jolly japes' — realistic mechanical mice, plastic flies, glasses of milk and beer that empty and then fill themselves up again, cigarettes that explode, squirt water or burn with unimaginably horrid pungency, 'holey spoons' that let the sugar run through them, spoons that break in half as you ply them, suckers that stick cups to their saucers, wine gums that burn like fire when you suck them, rubber chocolate biscuits and cakes and plastic cakes and plastic bacon and fried eggs — I wondered what manner of folk made up Mr. Bennett's clientele.

"All sorts," he told me. "Only last week a dignified old lady came in, looked round furtively, sidled up to the counter and whispered 'Have you any stink bombs?' Then there are young ladies who giggle so much that you can't hear what they want. A well-known city doctor comes in regularly for itching powder and a grey-haired bank-manager will buy anything that squirts water out of it. We even get nuns coming in here, and clergymen are among our best customers."

Just then a telephone began to ring. Mr Bennett didn't seem to hear it. "Your telephone," I said, "It's ringing."

"Oh, thanks. I'm a bit deaf," he smiled as he drew a rubber telephone-receiver from his jacket pocket and released his finger from the bellpush in his other pocket.

When I had recovered from that, he offered me a cigarette. I refused in the nicest possible way, thinking it safer to have one of my own. He pushed a box of matches across the counter to me. I picked it up and then dropped it again quickly, the pins and needles of an electric shock tingling in my arm.

Only one joke failed completely. It was a small telescope. "Take a peep through this," whispered Mr. Bennett conspiratorially. Gingerly I did so. I saw nothing. Nothing happened. "Must be something wrong with it," he said sadly.

Having made the purchases for my own party, I was about to take my leave. "If you're going to use those things on elderly people I think you ought to take a packet of this," advised Mr. Pilkington, "just in case they get too upset."

"Nervosin," said the label, "*Zur starkung schwacher Nerven. Pour fortifier les nerfs.* "I turned the packet over in my hand, there was a rustle and a gigantic spring bounded up in my face. I did *not* buy it.

I noticed people staring at me in the bus on the way home. "Whatever have you been up to?" my wife greeted me.

I loooked in the mirror. I had a perfect black eye. Then I remembered the telescope that hadn't worked.

6. THE WANING OF THE TWELFTH MOON
IN LIVERPOOL'S CHINATOWN

Things are not the same at *Sun Nien* since the bombs that razed Pitt Street tore the heart out of Liverpool's Chinatown.

Sun Nien is Chinese New Year. A movable feast, it fell this year, with the death of the Twelfth Moon, on January 31st, and long after we occidentals had put the last of our good resolutions on the shelf to gather dust for another cycle of the seasons, the folk from China who have made their home in that part of Liverpool which squats like a little piece of the Orient at the portals of the West, were busy preparing for the new start which the First Moon heralds.

★ ★ ★ ★

"Plenty long time now Chinese people no celeblate *Sun Nien* plopelly here," my old friend Tong Kin told me sadly as we sat together by the fire in the tiny Chinese grocery store, perfumed with the sharp aromas of suey sen and jagree dust and the sweet essence of areca-nut. "Once velly big feast."

Tong Kin has lived in Liverpool for all of thirty years. He was born in a little village in South China nearly seventy years ago and he has a veneration for *Sun Nien* that is rare to-day, for the modern expatriate Chinaman has become so thoroughly westernised that it is his invariable custom to observe the normal New Year of his adopted country.

Kung hi fat choy!

Good luck! A Happy New Year!

Old Tong Kin sucked at the black stem of his pipe and gazed into the fire. His eyes became dreamy and in a soft sing-song voice he began to talk wistfully of far-away New Year Days in far-away places. He talked in clipped uneasy English, but, sitting there on a tea-chest in that quiet dusty room, I seemed transported across green seas to a strange land of almond-blossom and brown earth, a land of alien pomp and pageantry.

China. New Year's Eve. The final preparations for the greatest feast of the year are under way. Everywhere the flick and flutter of brushes and dusters puts the dust to flight. The Twelfth Moon is on the wane. The Year of the Monkey dies. The Year of the Rooster crows to life. All must be clean and new when the new moon rises. Life begins again. The past is forgotten: dead as the vanished moon. The future unsullied: new-born. From midday the work of commerce has ceased. Shops are shuttered. In every house the decorations are going up. Gay-painted lanterns, streamers and banners of red silk. Red, by the way, is considered a very lucky colour in China, and

Chinese couples always wear something of that hue when they are getting married. (Curiously enough, it is blue that is regarded with favour at weddings in this country. "Something old, something new, something borrowed and something blue," decrees tradition.) Only the red dragon, Chinese equivalent of British red tape, is scorned! In the corner, ubiquitous at this season as our own Christmas tree, stands the New Year tangerine-tree, and entwined about are the lovely pink bells of the *tue chung* flower, so prized at New Year that a single bloom may cost anything between 100 and 300 dollars.

The moon wanes.

Evening aproaches and a great bath is filled with water in which quantities of leaves of the grapefruit-tree and handfuls of fragrant *shak kun fo* grass, gathered from the mountains, have been soaked. And fresh from this ceremonial bath, the Chinaman dresses himself from top to toe in new clothes. He sits down then to a huge feast, but as midnight approaches his mood becomes more austere, for New Year's Day must be observed with quiet rejoicing. On this first day of the First Moon no meat, nor anything which has had blood in it, must be eaten. There must be no swearing, no drinking of wine and nothing must be killed—not even a fly. There will be great family dinners, but the fare will be entirely vegetarian—fatchoy soup (made by boiling the lucky fatchoy seaweed in water), huge dishes of water-chestnuts, dry lilies, dry Chinese mushrooms, bamboo-shoots, bean-sprouts, bean curd, noodles and rice, helped down with plenty of soya sauce and followed by a dessert of lychees, longan and ginger and Chinese cheese and bowls of tea.

It wants but a few minutes to midnight now. The solitary red candle beneath the picture of Buddha will soon be lit. The match will set the jar of sandalwood curling its pungent smoke to the ceiling. The joss-sticks will glow and steam. In temple and family shrine the three little bowls of tea and the plate of cakes will be laid upon the votive table.

Kung hi fat choy!

Midnight.

Rap. Rap. Rap.

The firecrackers explode scaring the evil spirits away.

The steady yellow flame flowers from the candle top. This is the moment when the head of the house shuffles to the shrine and burns many, many pieces of paper scrawled with impossibly vast sums of money. A mock fortune goes up in smoke to propitiate the Gods of Fortune.

But all this belongs to the past. Even in China *Sun Nien* is a much more sober affair to-day, although the European visitor may find himself alarmed

23

by the fearsome firecrackers which drop, rip-rapping, from tenement tops into his rickshaw, or are hurled by mischievous boys into his car.

In Liverpool a few old Chinese families still follow a modified form of their ancient native customs, and here and there three bowls of tea and a guttering candle grace a little shrine, but there is no temple in this city, no official rejoicing and no firecrackers. On the other hand, practically all the Chinese families in Liverpool sit down on New Year's Eve to immense family dinners in traditionally decorated rooms and many Chinese restaurants provide special feasts for the members of their staffs. There are also gifts of money sent home to those who are still in China. These gifts are a very important feature of the New Year and a friend of mine in the catering business tells me that many Chinamen will happily plunge into debt in order to be able to send £30 or £40 home to their relations.

New Year's Day itself is a quiet one when friends and relatives visit one another and the children are given small sums of money carefully wrapped up in red paper. It is a day, too, of remembrance when gentle yellow fingers caress the ancestral tablets.

And now one more *Sun Nien* has come and gone.

For Tong Kin it was a day of memories.

He had taken one step nearer to that Paradise upon the verge of which he seems always to live.

He just sat by the fire, smoking and dreaming, waiting for the swallows to come, the almond to scatter its blossom upon him and the dew to make tears in the eye of the chrysanthemum.

7. THE SPANISH GARDEN

All in the blue Olympian weather it was difficult to realise that the little garden wasn't really in Spain; that the whole thing was an elaborate and wonderfully contrived make-believe on a scarred blitzed site in the sooted heart of Liverpool.

A shrine of beauty has arisen in Catherine Street—a tiny Eden in the brick-and-mortar wilderness—at which thousands of city workers gaze enraptured as they are borne past St. Philip Neri's Church on their green bus tops.

Sitting there in *El Jardin della Nuestra Senora*—The Garden of Our Lady—I chatted to the Reverend Dr. John Garvin, the man who conceived and carried out this amazingly imaginative piece of landscape transformation.

"It started," he told me, "as a bet. One day in 1952 I paid a visit to the Spanish roof-garden of Barker's Stores in London, and I made up my mind there and then that I would build my own Spanish garden in Liverpool. I said somewhat rashly perhaps, that I would have my blitzed site looking like a *jardin Espanol* within a year."

★　★　★　★

Dr. Garvin won his bet. But it was hard work transforming the brick and rubble strewn piece of waste land adjoining his church into the lush garden which burgeons there to-day, and the doctor had to take off his cassock, roll up his sleeves and get down to it in earnest.

Bit by bit, the ground was levelled off; ton after ton of good rich soil was shovelled into place; sunken paths were constructed and the fountains—twenty-five of them—began to play. Much ingenuity and little money had to be used. The kitchen sink of the bomb-razed house was made into a charming miniature alpine garden. Flower-tubs were knocked together out of old wine-casks and pipes of port—a process accompanied by much hilarity as the fumes which clung about them were still potent enough to make it a right merry business!

Most of the architectural features—roof and wall tiles, pillars, and the Moorish battlements of the walls—were fabricated with paint pot and cement by Dr. Garvin himself, but there were also certain importations from abroad, such as two magnificent marble columns, at least 2,000 years old, which, legend has it, came, via Lowther Castle, from the neighbourhood of the Roman Colosseum. There are too, several local antiquities: a fragment of a pillar from Gladstone's old house in Rodney Street, and two plump cherubim which have somehow winged their stony way here from the Bluecoat School.

And to this tranquil garden have come, during the last four years, beautiful things from all over the world: quartzite from distant Italian quarries, orange-trees from white-roofed Casablanca, delicate golden faience work from Vesselay and lovely painted tiles from Spain. We paused by a white-limed wall to admire a particularly fine tile from Bilbao, brightly embellished with a representation of the *Ovación y oreja*—the matador's final address to the pic-*ed* and banderillad bull.

★   ★   ★   ★

Appropriately enough in a priest's garden, there is a strongly religious motif running through it all. The centre-piece is a graceful shrine to the Madonna and Child and it is flanked by two specimens of the tree of heaven. The sacred symbol seven is represented by a yucca-tree, which flowers every seven years, and a flock of seven soul-white Aylesbury ducks. Alas! the latter have proved to be but whited sepulchres, for they have disgraced themselves by gobbling up all the carnations. For their sins, their number is being diminished as fast as the cook-pot will allow, and their place is to be taken by a columbarium of white fantails. Meanwhile, Jimmy the Mule (a kind of hybrid canary) sounds their knell on the little bell he tinkles for attention as you pass his swinging cage.

Close beside the garden well—"Some fool is bound to step into it," Dr. Garvin had said the day it was completed, and that very evening plunged knee-deep in it himself!—there is a greenhouse wherein grows a far-from-barren fig-tree, a flourish of vines and a proud cluster of passion-flowers. The priest climbed a rickety wooden ladder and, very gently, picked a single bloom. He held the little cerulean flower, which epitomises the tragic drama around which his church and his life have been built, tenderly in his hand and pointed out the instruments of Christ's Passion. They were all there: the three nails (the stigmas), the five wounds (the anthers), the crown of thorns (the red-stained rays of the corona), the scourge (a tendril tight-coiled as a watch-spring) and even the ten faithful apostles (the perianth)—Judas who betrayed and Peter who denied are missing.

It was as we were leaving this heavenly garden that I noticed the two green bay trees. "Yes," said Dr. Garvin, "they seem to like the climate of Catherine Street and flourish wickedly."

8. ELUSIVE UMBRELLAS AND TRUANT TEETH

The large, underground room was crowded with the rich harvest of Liverpool's absent-mindedness. I stood in the centre of a positive forest of umbrellas and let my eye wander over the serried ranks of suit-cases, the baskets of gloves, the strings of purses, the neat stacks of lunch-boxes, the shelves of books and the hampers of hats, caps, boots, shoes, belts, scarves and mackintoshes. People are getting more careless than ever with their possessions. That is the verdict of a man who should know, for he spends his life recording and docketing the things they lose and packing them away in the basement of 24, Hatton Garden, where the Liverpool Corporation Passenger Transport's Lost Property Office is situated. And believe me, it is a full time job, for the objects come pouring in at the rate of 150-200 a day, which represents a daily increase of up to 50 objects as compared with pre-war figures.

Generally speaking, the sort of things which turn up most frequently at Hatton Garden are gloves, umbrellas and purses, and, I was told, ladies' scarves are becoming more popular nowadays. Looking around, I was astonished at the bulk of some of the things that people have abandoned on city buses and trams. Wireless sets, bicycle wheels and a huge roll of wire netting, not to mention folding prams, which are coming in all the time. And then there are the more personal objects such as false teeth and glass-eyes which are quite common arrivals.

"What is the strangest piece of lost property that you have ever received?" I asked. The official thought for a moment or two. "Well, we once had a baby brought here," he said, "but we didn't waste much time in delivering it to the police." Apparently, it is not only inanimate objects which are abandoned with careless rapture. Only a month or two ago a pigeon was found on a bus. On another occasion it was a buzzing box full of bees and once, in the days of the trams, an ashen-faced conductor brought in a basket containing a fair-sized snake, which, it transpired, had been lost by a snake-charmer who was appearing at one of the local halls. For sheer impertinence it is difficult to beat the case of the abandoned parrot. This parrot, complete with cage, was left on the top of a tram, and when, a week or so later, its owner turned up to claim it, he blithely announced that he had "lost" the bird on purpose as he had been going away on holiday and felt certain that the L.C.P.T. would look after it well!

My informant then told me something which I never knew before. Every conductor is compelled by law to search his vehicle immediately before and after each journey for lost property. Everything which is found must be handed in by the conductor to the Hatton Garden office. It is retained there, and when its owner establishes his claim to it he has to pay a cloak-room

27

fee of 3d. per article for property not exceeding 2/- in value. An additional charge of one-twelfth of the agreed value of the piece of lost property, is levied, according to law, upon objects of greater value (subject to a maximum fee not in excess of £2), which sum is given as a reward to the conductor who found it.

Of course a great many of these things which are lost are never claimed, and the question of space, together with the perennial problem of moth, makes the disposal of the property an eventual necessity. This is effected by means of an auction sale which used to take place annually, but which is in future to be held every six months.

I went into the storeroom where the items were being assembled in readiness for the next sale, and there I found . . . a whole lot more umbrellas! Umbrellas of every shape and size, neatly stacked on shelves, their multi-coloured handles making a charming pattern. I noticed in particular one with a beautifully carved head of a dog. The poor thing looked quite lonely and forlorn. More than 10,000 umbrellas a year pass through these rooms and that is nothing compared with what it used to be. "I think fewer people carry them these days." said the official, "and those who do are more careful with them. They are so expensive now." Then he told me the story of the lady who lost her umbrella in a tram one morning. She came to the office and recovered it. Later that afternoon she lost it again. Back she came. and was lucky enough to get it back—only to leave it in a tram again that same night! She returned for the third time next morning, and there was her brolly, which must have had the instinct of a homing-pigeon, waiting for her. Is this, one is tempted to ask, a record?

Leaving Hatton Garden, I went down the road to Dale Street where, in a large room across the courtyard of the Main Bridewell, the Liverpool City Police have their own Central Lost Property Office. It is to this place that all the things which are found in the streets are brought by honest folk—there is a surprising number of them—who do not hold with that dishonest maxim that finding is keeping.

The picture here was rather different from that at the L.C.P.T. office. Commonest objects were purses, keys, handbags, shopping bags and spectacles. Truant false teeth came in pretty regularly but umbrellas were comparatively rare. There were, however, a great many monstrous lorry wheels, bales of cloth, sacks of potatoes and suchlike, which fall off lorries, especially in the Dock Road area. Again, the things people lose made extaordinary hearing. Throughout the years, wigs, false hands, artificial arms and legs, and even a slightly gruesome casket containing somebody's ashes, have been handed in.

Downstairs there are five large cellars and a strong-room crammed with the crop of carelessness gathered from Liverpool's streets. Frequently, valuable jewellery, watches and rings, sometimes worth hundreds of pounds, are brought here. The police make no charge for their services except in the case of property left in taxis, when, as prescribed by the law, a fee of one shilling in the pound on the value of the object, is payable. This sum is handed to the taxi-driver by way of reward. There is, however, an inconspicuous box upon the counter for contributions to the Liverpool District Police Orphanage, and many people like to celebrate their good fortune by making a small donation to a very worthy cause.

Occasionally, practical jokers leave parcels in the street, which, upon investigation, prove to contain no more valuable lost property than an obscene mass of tea-leaves and egg-shells! Late one evening an extremely excited gentleman rushed in bearing a very important looking envelope, its flaps all red sealing-wax and with "£100" prominently marked upon its face. Breathlessly, he explained that he had just found it in the street and did not want the responsibility of keeping it overnight. The envelope was opened and in it was found a carefully folded newspaper.

All lost property delivered to the police is kept for at least twelve months unless, after three months have elapsed, the finder claims it. He must, however, sign a form of indemnity before he is allowed to take it away. If it is not claimed, either by the owner or the finder, the property is, after the official period of time has elapsed, sold by public auction.

Once again I asked my question about the strangest object ever to have passed through that limbo of the lost and found. "We had a skeleton once," said the police-officer, "a medical student must have lost it. But I think this takes some beating," and his eyes twinkled as from a dark recess below the counter he produced a brand-new bed-pan!

I had gone a good hundred yards down Dale Street when I missed my umbrella. Shame-facedly, I turned and made my way back to the Lost Property Office.

9. PILLAR TO POST

P.B. No.114 stands where the short dagger of Sefton Park Road thrusts at the sabre-curve of Croxteth Road. To the casual observer there is nothing to mark this very ordinary Edward VII period pillar-box as in any way different from any of the other 888 pillar-boxs which colourfully punctuate the grey pavements of the Liverpool Head Postmaster's area. But it is, in fact, a kind of ancient monument, standing as it does just a little to the east of the site of Liverpool's very first pillar-box. The story of this pioneer pillar-box goes back to the days of the Crimean War; to November 1854, to be precise. At that time, when British postal reformer, Sir Roland Hill, was still trying to persuade the Commissioners of Paving in London to approve pillar-boxes for the metropolis, the enterprising Liverpool postmaster gave an order to a local firm of iron-founders for a hollow cast-iron pillar, having a letter-slit on one side, and with a small door on the other, through which a letter-box could be inserted and removed. So it came about that, months before London saw its first pillar-box, the people of Liverpool's Sefton Park district were making regular use of one.

Just over a century ago, the pillar-box was only a traveller's tale in Britain. On the Continent, street mail-boxes had long been established. They probably derived from the invention of that nameless official of sixteenth-century Italy who fitted-up closed boxes, known as *Tamburi*, outside the churches of the Florentine Republic wherein could be placed, in safe anonymity, denunciations of State enemies.

In England, however, letters had to be taken to official receiving houses for despatch. These places were far from numerous, and closed at an early hour in the afternoon. Urgent or late correspondence had to be handed to the bellman, a picturesque figure in a top-hat, scarlet swallow-tail coat and blue trousers, who had originally been employed by an eighteenth-century worthy, Charles Povey, who once ran his own halfpenny postal service. The bellman was really a kind of perambulating pillar-box. He used to parade the streets, ringing a handbell and carrying a locked bag provided with a slit for inserting letters, which, for a fee of one penny each, he would deliver to the central office. The bellman disappeared from the scene in 1846 when the receiving-houses were ordered to remain open until 7 p.m.

It was as part of his plans for the reform of British postal services that Roland Hill had, by 1840, suggested the adoption of pillar letter-boxes similar to those which he had seen in France. He managed to obtain approval for one to be installed in Westminster Hall, but the official side was not at all happy at the idea of "allowing precious missives to be committed to the interiorof an unprotected box situated on the public footpath."

In 1851, in response to a request by the people of St. Helier, Jersey,

30

for the number of town receiving-houses to be increased, an assistant post-office surveyor was sent to the Channel Islands. That surveyor was none other than Anthony Trollope, of Barsetshire fame, and it was as a result of his recommendations that, on November 23rd, 1852, the first roadside letter-boxes in Great Britain were erected—four on Jersey and three on Guernsey. These first boxes were four feet in height, they were of cast-iron, red in colour, and stood on a granite pedestal. Originally, they were hexagonal in shape, but they were later made octagonal by the insertion of two extra panels. They were an unqualified success from the start, and in March 1854, experimental pillar-boxes were erected at Cheltenham. By the September of that year, officialdom was at long last satisfied as to the suitability of the new amenities, and in 1855 London received its first six pillar-boxes. In the following year fifty new boxes were ordered, eleven of which went to Edinburgh, where they were hailed with such enthusiasm that before the interior fittings were complete they were filled to overflowing with mail!

Contrary to general expectation, early pillar-boxes were not abused, although street-urchins displayed a tendency to try and fill them up with sticks and stones and, from the first, November 5th brought its crop of pillar-box fires! Nevertheless, they have sometimes been found to contain other things than letters. Pickpockets have been known to place wallets and purses in them after they have extracted the money, and in rural districts postmen have found birds nesting in them. A colony of snails once took up residence in one and used the letters for food. An unsolved mystery was the discovery of a cat and her kittens snugly ensconed among the letters!

During the twenty years following the installation of the first pillar-boxes, many different types were used. London's earliest half-dozen had proved unsatisfactory. They were all square, squat, heavy, iron contraptions, painted green and crowned with a fretted dome and an iron ball. Each bore a plate showing the distance to the General Post-Office and, on the sides, the legend "Post-Office Letter-box." Their appearance was not good and they were too low. The indicator plates were constantly splashed with mud, and, even when clean, it was necessary to kneel on the pavement in order to read them.

The public poured in designs for new pillar-boxes, ranging from clock-towers to sign-posts. In 1856, hexagonal boxes, crusted with those brass ornamentations dear to the Victorian heart, and embellished with a compass-plate on the top, enjoyed a brief vogue. In the early days, blue, brown, green, bronze and yellow-painted boxes were employed indiscriminately,though green ones predominated. But in 1874, red was adopted as the standard colour, and now a special weather-resistant red paint, prepared from a carefully preserved formula, coats every pillar-box. Blue-painted boxes for the reception of air-mail letters joined the familiar red ones in 1930, but by 1938 the bulk of foreign mail was going by air, and the special boxes were withdrawn. In war time, pillar-boxes suddenly acquired bright yellow hats. This was due, however, to the fact that they were painted with a substance which reacted to the presence of gas, and was not for decorative purposes.

The year 1876 saw the introduction of the plain cylindrical box which has come to be the standard type mainly because it is more econmical to maintain. Modern pillar-boxes are made in four styles. Three of these are cylindrical, single-aperture boxes, weighing 7½ cwt., and one is an oval, double-fronted type, which weighs 19 cwt. There are also some eleven kinds of lamp and wall-boxes. Today, there are about 90,000 pillar, wall and lamp-boxes in the United Kingdom. That is approximately one to every 450 yards in urban districts, and one to every half-mile in populated country areas. Pillar-boxes are preferred, except where traffic is too small to warrant their erection, as they hold 800 letters, as compared with a mere 400 which is the maximum capacity of a wall-box.

The ordinary pillar-box is made of cast-iron. It is constructed in three sections, the cap, the door and the pillar, which are bolted together. The strong locks which are fitted to the doors have been made for over sixty years by one well-known firm, and the time-of-collection plates have also been made by one firm for nearly forty years. It was in Liverpool that the movable tablets which show the time of the next collection were first used. Invented by Mr. J. D. Rich, appointed Liverpool Postmaster in 1875, the device was intended not only for the convenience of the public, but also as a check on the activities of the postman. It is interesting to note that pillar-boxes, which are said to be immovable, are planted only eighteen inches in the ground, but they are bedded in concrete.

Although the average life of a pillar-box is assessed as being in the region of forty years, many Liverpool ones are of much greater age. Round about 1862 it was noticed that some pillar-boxes bore no evidence of being post-office property, so an experimental design, bearing a large crown on top, was manufactured, and six of these were erected in Liverpool. One was placed outside St. George's Hall in 1863. It was later moved to the front of Lime Street Post-Office, where it continued in use until 1938. A second, stood formerly in Exchange Flags, whence it was removed in 1938 when alterations were being made. It is now in the Post-Office Museum in London. Three crowned pillar-boxes still remain, however. One stands in Sheil Road, near the entrance to Newsham Park; one is situated at the junction of Breck and Everton Roads, and the third occupies the corner of St. Anne Street and Queen Anne Street. They are, all three, museum-pieces, strangely antiquated-looking in their present-day settings of busy streets, where, throughout six reigns, they have stood guard over countless sackfuls of Royal Mail.

10.   IN A MAGIC CIRCLE

Whatever their magic powers, they did not, I ruefully reflected as I drove through a blinding rainstorm to a meeting of the Liverpool Magic Circle, exercise any influence over the elements.

My objective was Lynwood Hall in Rice Lane, Walton, where, once a month, a coven of twentieth-century warlocks convenes for a *Walpurgis* night of unmitigated magic.

Actually, I was very honoured to receive an invitation from the President, Mr. Owen Jones, to be present at one of these sorcerous sessions, for the Liverpool Magic Circle is on the strictly secret list, and I was the first non-magician guest ever to be permitted to take part in the proceedings.

Founded in 1951, the Liverpool Magic Circle is a very exclusive brotherhood of magi, whose membership is rigidly restricted to thirty. Its members are recruited from all departments of life. During the day, they may masquerade successfully as clerks, accountants, bank officials, commercial travellers, motor mechanics, post-office workers, press photographers and shop assistants, but when the fingers of the clock point the witching hour of release from the bondage of shop and office they are magically transformed into mystics.

It was shortly after 8-30 when I found myself in the uncurtained pitch and pinewood hall where some twenty magicians were awaiting me and where I promptly commited a serious breach of wizard's etiquette by referring to them as conjurers. Apparently, that word is absolutely taboo in magic circles; its use is tantamount to calling the Philharmonic Orchestra a band. They are MAGICIANS, and, by the way, they do not do tricks, but perform a "routine" of "effects."

The proceedings commenced with a bang—literally.

Sensible of the dangers which lurked in such surroundings, I hung on to my hat (it was a new one and I didn't want it to be spirited away by magic or any other less reputable method) and I sat down gingerly upon the chair to which I was escorted, half afraid that it might collapse. It did not and I began to recover my self-confidence. Nothing untoward had happened so far, and I was smugly congratulating myself that there were no flies on me when they brought me the visitors' book. I opened it. There was a terrific explosion and I fell off the chair. Endeavouring to laugh that one off, I accepted the pen which was profferred to me, pulled off the cap and there was another deafening report. With a sickly smile and a shaking hand, I scrawled my signature in the book with as much dignity as I could muster after jumping three feet in the air.

After that they took pity on me, for Mr. John Deacon, producing a piece of dark green cloth, upon which was inscribed in large white lettering "NO

BEER," rolled it into a funnel-like shape and poured from its apparently empty interior a glass of beer which, magic or otherwise, tasted very good to me.

Mr. Ray Dyson, a mental magician—that description does not imply any lack of balance in Mr. Dyson, but simply means that he specializes in psychological magic, thought-reading and prediction—was the next to take the stage. He asked me to go onto the platform and invited me to select any card from a perfectly new pack, the seal of which he broke. I did so, marked the card with my initials and sealed it in an envelope. I was then told to open another envelope which had been sent through the post to me *two days previously.* It proved to contain a note from Mr. Dyson which read, "You will select the Queen of Hearts." I then opened the envelope containing the marked card which I had just picked from the pack. Sure enough it *was* . . . the Queen of Hearts. At the end of the effect I was very generously presented with the brand-new pack of cards.

So far, I had done very nicely out of the evening. I had received a glass of beer and a pack of cards. But it wasn't to be all beer and playing-cards; now, something was demanded of me—a ten shilling note. Not surprisingly, the man who wanted my money was a bank official, Mr. Don Gilroy (appropriately enough, treasurer of the Circle), who, like others in his profession—my bank-manager in particular—seemed intent on making me poorer. With misgivings, I handed him the note, which he promptly burned. Now most of my money goes up in smoke anyway, but I like to be the one who enjoys the warmth of its cremation. This was extremely disconcerting. But I needn't have worried. Five minutes later, the ten-shilling note was reproduced safe and sound from the interior of a stout, locked box.

The President, Mr. Owen Jones, then performed a neat little essay in levitation. A lighted candle was placed in a tall, glass funnel, both previously examined, the candle and funnel were put down on a table, and, after sundry magic passes and unintelligible exhortations, the candle was induced to rise six inches in the air. How that was done I just can't begin to guess. All I *do* know is that there were no wires because I searched for them.

One effect which gave me especial delight was Mr. Richard Satterley's magic plate. Mr. Satterley led me onto the stage, gave me a little hammer and told me to smash up a white dinner-plate. Usually, I do this at home without being invited when I am helping with the washing-up, and get the rounds of the kitchen from my aggrieved wife. On this occasion, therefore I set to work with a will and soon reduced the plate to fragments. The pieces were scooped into a bag and one small portion of china was given to me as a souvenir. "Sim Sala Bim!" the bag was empty; a flash, and there, on the far side of the stage, was the plate, fully restored except for one triangular chip. The piece in my hand fitted exactly into it.

Then, Mr. Charles Green, forty-five years a magician, gave a demonstration of hypnotism. Three of us submitted to the experiment. My two companions were soon in a trance, but, I regret to report, I proved unresponsive to the "fluence," and was told that I am not susceptible to hypnosis.

I'm not so sure about that though, for it was at that point in the meeting that I almost lost my head. Mr. Roy Pilkington, the Vice-President, produced a fearsome guillotine and invited me to be decapitated. In a moment of bravado, I accepted, and mounted the steps to the stage feeling much as Sydney Carton must have felt when he walked to his execution in *A Tale of Two Cities*. Mr. Pilkington thrust a carrot into the slot of his alarming instrument. There was a rumble, the glint of light on a wicked-looking knife and the carrot was cut clean in half. The executioner smiled menacingly at me. I paled and started thinking of tumbrils and hags who went on knitting as the head of another "aristo" fell into the bloodstained basket. In vain I pointed out that there would be no one to write about the proceedings if they beheaded me. I was led to the guillotine; I knelt down; my neck was put in the slot; the moment of truth was upon me. Then it happened. The blade thundered down, I closed my eyes and felt the sweat trickling behind my ears. A few seconds later I was being helped to my feet, and, miracle of miracles, my head was still on my shoulders.

Never was a drink more welcome. It mattered not that Mr. Bill Thompson produced it by mixing equal quantities of vinegar, salt and rice in a cocktail-shaker, the resulting "Green Goddess" was exactly right for the restoration of a reprieved man. Just how shattered I had been by my experience on the guillotine may be deduced from the fact that I even forgot to inquire of Mr. Thompson exactly what you had to do to contrive so delicious a cocktail from such economical and unpromising ingredients.

When at length I was myself again, the President intimated that I was to become an honorary magician. I was given a magic wand—which disintegrated in my hand—three coloured balls and a corruscating cylinder. I was instructed to place the cylinder on the table and drop the balls into it. I had then to wave my wand over it and pronounce certain cabalistic words. I did as I was bid, lifted the cylinder, and . . . there were the three balls! Everyone roared with laughter: I blushed scarlet and tried again. The result was the same. By this time my blood was up and I determined to have a third try. More wand-wavings, frantic incantations, and when I lifted the cylinder again, lo and behold, the balls had completely vanished. Merlin has nothing on me, but if anyone asks me how it is done, the answer is—just magic!

11. TIME ON HIS HANDS

"A Tompion," said the old clockmaster, "is to the horologist what a Stradivarius is to a violinist." And I gathered that it is just about as rare. "In all Liverpool," he went on, "there is, to the best of my knowledge, only one genuine Tompion, grandfather-clock. It stands in the board room of Messrs. Owen Owen's store, and it is worth, I should say, every penny of £1,500."

Thomas Tompion (Born 1639. Died 1713) was the greatest grandfather-clock maker England ever produced. Even in that elect company of 17th and 18th century craftsmen which includes such literally time-honoured names as Edward East, Joseph Knibb, Daniel Quare, Christopher Gould and Joseph Windmills, his is a name that shines bright beyond the rest, and specimens of his work command the highest respect, and the highest prices, among collectors.

"You know," said Mr. H. A. Wollen, the clock maker, "if anyone was to bring a Tompion into my shop and entrust me with the repairing of it I should feel it to be the greatest compliment that he could possibly pay me. They are really wonderful clocks and some of the finest movements are such masterpieces of precision and economy that they only need winding once a year. As a matter of fact I *have* on one or two occasions had people bring in what they believed were Tompions, but they have always turned out to be fakes. Anyway, there are far more alleged Tompions in the antique shops than one man could possibly have made. And here's a curious thing: several times I have handled clocks by anonymous makers with mechanisms so exquisite that I am inclined to think that they *were* genuine Tompions."

My friend the clock maker is, as you will probably have gathered, a real enthusiast, and a visit to his little shop, which seems filled with the whispering spirit of Time, is a most interesting experience. All around you stand the venerable grandfathers muttering to themselves, deep and throaty, high and querulous, wheezy and asthmatical, each according to his age and condition. Here is a big fat Victorian clock which reminds the clock maker of an old shawl woman: there, an elegant slip of a clock that represents to him a slender refined lady. "They all have personalities," he will tell you. "Every clock has its own unmistakable individuality and many of them remind me of people that I know." And he gives them nicknames and when they are sold he almost feels as if he has lost a friend. "Now there was one clock that I used to call 'Cheerful Joe'. A real merry little grandfather that was. It had such a happy strike and such a pleasant dial. Another I had was downright sinister. A huge thing, all carved black oak and with a figure

36

of an angel painted on the dial. The eyes of the angel moved from side to side and his lips opened and closed. It gave me the creeps and made me think of funerals every time I looked at it. I was quite relieved when I sold it."

The physiognomy of grandfather-clocks is a subject in itself. Early specimens were relatively uncomplicated, boasting only brass or silvered faces, though these were sometimes ornately engraved. Mr. Wollen showed me a beautiful example, dated 1760, with a lovely engraving of Cinderella trying on the slipper. Towards the end of the 18th century it became the fashion to provide the grandfathers with enamel faces and to paint little scenes in the corners. The 19th century went a step farther and introduced various novelties in the form of moving parts—ships that rocked backwards and forwards as though tossed upon the timeless ocean of eternity, windmills whose sails were blown by the breath of Time, a lion pouncing upon Daniel, its great red eyes revolving most fearsomely, and even a complete Punch and Judy show with moving figures. Some decorations were conceived in more utilitarian vein—a smiling man in the moon whose position denoted lunar phases and ages; an illuminated inset which showed the day of the month; an artistic seascape in which the level of the painted waves rose and fell in relation to high and low tides. Among the old Liverpool clock makers (men like Park, Lassell and John Wyke, who lived in Wyke's Court on the site of what is now the city's main bridewell) it was a frequent practice to further embellish the top of the dials with fragments of clock-face philosophy—'On Time's uncertain day Eternity depends', 'Time shows the way of Life's decay'; 'The man is yet unborn that can duly weigh an hour'; and the stern call to the sluggard, 'Awake! Arouse each active power and not in idle dreams lose this little hour.'

And when you come to think of it, is it any wonder that clock makers are philosophical men, for do they not spend all of their lives within earshot of the measured passing of the soul of Time? Yet strangely enough their senses, if not their sensibilities, become deafened, for Mr. Wollen told me that he is so accustomed to the tickings and the strikings that he never hears them. But what he *does* hear is the silence when a clock stops! This I can well appreciate, for, some years ago, I bought a grandfather-clock. The thing had been going ever since the Battle of Waterloo, but such is my evil star that a month or two after its arrival it stopped dead. When first it came to share my home its chimes used regularly to wake me up. After a few weeks, however, they became part of the sound-pattern of my life, and when the time of its muteness came I would start awake night after night, my ears straining for the familiar bell-notes of the hours. Nor was unbroken sleep mine again until my moribund grandfather had been revivified.

★ ★ ★ ★

37

In the little workroom where the clock maker restores like a surgeon the ailing entrails of his clocks, I met Williams. Williams, a plump ginger tom, ten years old now and still sporting a disgracefully ragged ear acquired in the days of his courtship, is no ordinary cat. A clock maker's familiar maybe, not only does he refrain from playing with the pendulums (surely a terrible temptation), hear the calls of sundry cuckoos without so much as the flicker of a whisker or the flexing of a claw, but if Mr. Wollen should happen to drop some tiny vital of a clock's mechanism Williams will always retrieve it and push it towards his master with his paw.

All in all, the clock maker is a happy, easy-going man who loves his work. His one grief is that of late years the grandfather-clock has fallen into disfavour. "Too big for modern homes," he told me sadly. That is why so many of them now are relegated to the cemetery of the sale-room. Every so often he will go along and rescue some forlorn grandfather (bids sometimes mount no higher than 7s. 6d.), and he is never so happy as when, after hours of patient work, he sees its old heart begin to pulse again with life. To him the voice of a clock is the finest music in the world and it is only in a business connotation that he fails to find beauty in the word "tick"!

12. LADY HOUSTON SLEPT HERE

As soon as the manager switched on the light I saw that the Tower Triplets were safely in bed.

Outside, a thin grey wind drove a sea-drizzle of rain against the red brick walls of New Brighton Tower. But here in the dust-sheeted waxworks, the three zany figures, surrounded by bottles of beer and with a large barrel of stout—from which a rubber tube snaked down into the ever-open mouth of the thirstiest of the sleepers—suspended above their bed, lay peacefully awaiting the time when the Easter bells should summon the laughing crowds to the Tower fairground.

It was not, however, the comic sleepers, but the bed they slept in that I had come to see. It had for me something of that queer magnetism which draws the gaping hordes to contemplate the chair in which Branwell Brontë got regularly drunk, the table that King Henry the Eighth threw his discarded chicken bones on, or, less innocently, the spade with which Dr. Crippen dug his victim's grave. For that vast and rather abominable bed of brass and inlaid mother-of-pearl had, I was assured, however improbably, once belonged to Lady Fanny Lucy Houston.

★ ★ ★ ★

Who to-day recalls the rococo figure of Lady Houston? Born just a hundred years ago in Lower Kennington Green, she was the daughter of a London warehouseman named Thomas Radmall. From small beginnings as a cockney chorus-girl, Lucy Radmall progressed through three marriages to become the contender for the title of not only the richest, but also the dottiest, woman in England.

Her first two essays in matrimony—to Theodore Brinckman and the 9th Lord Byron—having ended in divorce and death respectively, she married for the third time in 1924. Her new husband was Sir Robert Houston, the Liverpool shipping magnate, and he survived his nuptials only two years.

Thus, at the age of 69, she found herself alone and in possession of a vast fortune of £5,000,000, and seemed set fair for a quiet and dignified old age. But it didn't work out quite like that.

During the last ten years of her life the woman whose noble work in running a home for tired nurses during the First World War had earned her the distinction of becoming one of the first five Dame Commanders of the Order of the British Empire, went suddenly haywire.

Politics were her undoing. She developed a taste for abusing politicians whom she accused of betraying the Empire to the Bolsheviks. The favourite victims of her witch-hunting were Messrs. Baldwin, Ramsay MacDonald and the young Anthony Eden. Her dislike of Sir Samuel Hoare amounted to a positive mania, and when he was standing at a by-election in Chelsea she enlivened the hustings with a troupe of nigger minstrels. The minstrels, carefully rehearsed beforehand in her bedroom, where "she lay, her still-blonde curls peeping out from under a red, white and blue turban, beating time with a lorgnette," sang political parodies to the tunes of popular comic songs at all 'Slippery Sam's' meetings.

In 1933 she bought *The Saturday Review*, provided it with a garish red, white and blue cover, and used it not only as platform for her political campaign, but also to disseminate the details of her patent cold cure! On the back page were printed, week after week, full directions for the taking, both up the nose and down the gullet, of this odious nostrum (compounded of castor-oil, Byans oil, Listerine, cinnamon and vast quantities of yellow Vaseline), together with the request that, in lieu of payment, the reader would say "God Bless Lady Houston" after dosing himself.

She took an active part in the production of her paper and was often to be seen outside the printer's on press days, sitting in her Rolls-Royce, a magnificent fur coat over her nightdress, surrounded by page-proofs, bottles of stout and cans of yellow Vaseline.

Later the same year her 1,571-ton steam-yacht, *Liberty,* was to be seen in Poole Harbour, an illuminated sign slung from its 80-foot mast blazoning in coloured electric bulbs "THE PRIME MINISTER IS A TRAITOR".

Her 1st public appearance was in connection with the abdication of King Edward VIII, whom she venerated. In a final frenzy of patriotic fervour she abstained from both eating and sleeping, and expired peacefully in her 80th year after a touching session of hymn-singing.

Wondering how it came about that anything so intimate as her eccentric ladyship's bed came to be in a New Brighton waxworks, I made a few enquiries and discovered that Sir Robert Houston was one of the prime movers in the scheme which, in 1895, gave New Brighton its tower and recreation ground. He was, moreover, the owner of Rock Point Castle, a large old house in the tower grounds, and it was from here that this formidable bed was salvaged. I can't help feeling that its present odd function is quite in keeping with its early history—even down to the surrounding bottles of beer!—and was it only imagination that seemed to detect the approving spirit of Lady H. herself hovering above the shining brass curtain-rails?

13. DEATH IN THE AFTERNOON

Speke Airport.
Whit Monday, 21st May, 1956.
For once the weather is idyllic.
A shimmering haze of heat blankets the bank-holiday crowd of 100,000 who have come to see the International Air Display.
The sun blazes, a blinding white-hot brazier, its brilliance stabbing off the sleek silver bodies of the planes that buzz like angry gnats through the tepid air.
The sky is Mediterranean-blue, the tarmac and terminal buildings gleam a painful Tangier-white, the grass of the airfield is scorched yellowish-brown in patches.
Children squeal with delight. Mother brings out the flask and sandwiches. Father smokes his pipe and, sprawling on the warm earth, watches the flashing aerobats through field-glasses.
The Sipa 200 Minijet zooms low. A gasp scythes across the field. The crowd involuntarily ducks—recovers to a ripple of shame-faced laughter.
On such a day it is good to be alive, but for one of the 100,000, all unsuspected, death is quietly waiting in that azure vault of sky.
Very soon now the great event of the pageant is scheduled to take place. Thousands of programmes rustle an overture of anticipation. There is a pleasant mounting of tension.
The cause of all this excitement is a slight, swarthy, 37-year-old Frenchman, Léo Valentin, who, ever since he was a small boy watching the storks and buzzards soaring above the trees of the great park that surrounded his home at Epinal in the Vosges department of France, has devoted his life to the dream of flying like a bird.
This afternoon is to see the climax of that dream for, billed as the Bird Man, he is to jump from an aircraft at 8,500 feet and, with the aid of a pair of wooden wings, attempt to glide for several miles before parachuting down onto the airfield.
Already once to-day Valentin has launched himself into space. An hour earlier he has executed a brilliant delayed parachute drop, plummeting from 8,000 feet before, just 1,000 feet above the ground, he pulled his rip-cord and with a sharp crack the billowing, white silk of his parachute blossomed out to brake his 120 m.p.h. free fall and float him at a safe 15 m.p.h. to the reassuring earth.
But *this* is his hour.
He is the last of the twentieth-century disciples of Icarus.
He is to try and realise the age-old dream of the ancient Greek, and like him he is to lose his wings.

41

He is to challenge the sky—and lose.

★　★　★　★

Léo Valentin was born of humble parents at Epinal in 1919. Before he was ten, fascinated by aeroplanes, he was spending most of his time wandering around the hangars of Dogneville Aerodrome, gazing enraptured at the quaint flying-machines and sometimes actually talking to those leather-suited and goggled demigods, the pilots who flew them.

He left school at sixteen to become, first, a butcher's boy and then an apprentice locksmith, but the urge to fly persisted, and he scraped together sufficient money to attend lectures at the Vosges Air Club in his spare time.

In 1938, at the age of 19, he enlisted in the *Armée de l'Air*, was sent to Blida in North Africa and rapidly rose to the rank of corporal, but impatient at the prospect of the three years' pilot's course which one had to take before starting to fly, he volunteered to train as a parachutist at the Maison Blanche centre at Algiers. He made his first jump over Baraki on October 15th, 1938.

The following year war was declared and the French parachutists were for a time transformed into mountain troops, but subsequently continued their training at Montélimar.

Valentin was on the Pyrenean frontier when France fell, but he managed to escape, via the underground, to North Africa. There he joined the parachute school which had been formed at Fez and, with more than 80 jumps to his credit now, he was promptly made a sergeant-instructor.

Presently, however, the monotony of camp life began to bore him. He wanted action. And so, at the end of 1942, he embarked on a troop-transporter, and a few days later found himself in Liverpool.

From there he was sent straightaway to a camp near Glasgow where the British Special Air Service was undergoing intensive training in preparation for the invasion.

On June 9th, 1944, Valentin parachuted into Brittany. He dropped over Morbihan and, after blowing up the railway lines between Vannes and Rennes, made his way to the St. Marcel Plateau.

During the next few months he took part in some fierce fighting and, after a brief respite back in England, he was sent into the Loire pocket where in the course of an engagement with the S.S. his right arm was shattered by an explosive bullet. He was treated in the hospital at Issoudun and convalesced on the Marne and in England.

At the end of the war Valentin was promoted to sergeant-major and posted as an instructor to the parachute school at Lannion. A few months later the school was transferred to Pau, and there Valentin remained until he decided to quit the *Armée de l'Air* in 1949.

It was in the Pau Library that Valentin first began to pore over certain ancient books in which was embalmed the history of man's long fight to conquer the heavens.

He read, with mounting excitement, of the pioneer parachutists; of old Fausto Veranzio, the Venetian mathematician who, in 1616, first described an apparatus resembling a parachute; of Sebastien le Normand, the father of parachuting; of Garnerin; Berry, the first parachutist to be launched from a plane; Pégoud; and the American, Irvin, who, on April 28th, 1919, jumped from an aeroplane flying at 1,800 feet and opened his parachute at 600 feet, thus accomplishing the first delayed action drop.

He read and he resolved . . . he would have *his* place in the sky.

This ambition was achieved on March 23rd, 1948, when he jumped over Pau from a height of 22,000 feet, allowing himself to fall to 1,800 feet before opening his parachute. That exploit put the world record for a free drop without a respirator in his pocket. The following November he established a new world record for a free drop without respirator by night.

During those four years at Pau Valentin made one other great advance. He invented a method of controlling his position during a free fall. After a considerable amount of perilous experimentation the Valentin position was born.

Naturally, all these activities had made Léo Valentin something of a star in the world of aviation, and when he retired from the *Armée de l'Air* he made up his mind to go in for stunt parachuting. It was now that he began to consider again the whole question of flight. He wanted to fly like a bird, and so he decided that, like a bird, he must sprout wings.

Working in secret, he made himself a pair of canvas wings. He tried them out on April 30th, 1950, at Villacoublay before a crowd of 300,000. They were not a success and nearly cost him his life. Nevertheless, he attempted a second flight with them over Meaux-Esbly Airfield on May 4th. Once again they proved unsatisfactory. Convinced by these two experiences, Valentin realised that he must abandon canvas wings. What he really needed, he told himself, were wooden feathers.

Throughout the last six months of 1950 and the first six months of 1951, Valentin and his friend Monsieur Collignon spent many, many hours in the latter's workshops on the outskirts of Paris constructing a pair of wooden wings.

Valentin made his first test jump with them at Cormeilles-en-Vexin on June 8th, 1951. He launched himself from a platform attached to the side of a helicopter. A terrific gust of wind closed the wings and he got into a terrible spin. He only just managed to pull out of it and landed with the hard-won knowledge that some way must be devised to prevent the wings from closing.

43

A month later, his wings now provided with automatic locks, the indomitable little Frenchman was ready to try again.

This occasion—July 2nd, 1951—was for him a rather special one, for the venue of the jump was that same Dogneville Airfield where, nearly a quarter of a century before, the young Valentin had watched and envied those heroes of the sky. He soared up to 9,000 feet in a Junkers 52 and leapt into the void. He had just time to glimpse the well-remembered landscape of his childhood spread like a tawny map below him, and then . . . he found himself plunged into a bewildering spin. The lock of his right wing had been damaged. The left wing was firm, locked, but the right hung limp and flapping at his side. The spin intensified. The earth whirled like a vortex. The blood rushed to his head. His vision blurred. On the point of fainting he just managed by a gigantic effort of will to pull the rip-cord. Trembling like a leaf, he landed on the very brink of the Moselle. It was the worst drop he had ever made.

It says much for the man's nerve that after an experience like that Valentin could ever again entrust himself to the tender mercies of those fickle wings. But victory was just around the corner. Three years later, on May 13th, 1954, at Gisy-les-Nobles, near Pont-sur-Yonne, Léo Valentin, the Bird Man, using his wooden wings, 'flew' for a distance of at least three miles over Thorigny and landed safe and sound in a field of lucerne.

Now, two years later almost to the day, on May 21st, 1956, at Speke, Liverpool, Valentin is to experiment with a new pair of wings. They are of bright orange-coloured balsa-wood. Four feet high, and with an overall span of 9 feet, they are attached to a light metal alloy corset and fitted with ailerons. The whole apparatus weighs 28 lb.

The Bird Man is to fly again and I am to fly with him.

★　★　★　★

It is 3-40 p.m. precisely.

I follow the diminutive figure of the Bird Man across the tarmac and clamber after him into the waiting Dakota.

Five minutes later the engines are revving up.

We begin to taxi slowly out to the runway.

"Un moment! Un moment!" shouts Valentin.

He has forgotten something.

He leaps out, runs across the tarmac to a small shed.

A minute or so later he is back with a box spanner.

He makes a last-minute adjustment to his left wing.

We move off again.

At 3-55 we roar along the field. The ground drops away.

We are airborne.

44

We bank out over the River Mersey, describe a vast circle over Cheshire, climb steadily to 9,000 feet. The earth is spread out below us like a green patchwork quilt. It looks far away. Very harmless. The late afternoon sun glints gold across great cotton-woolly patches of cumulus cloud bunched like irregular icebergs in a blue and misty sea of sky.

It is cold in the plane. Icy air comes rushing in through the 7-foot gap where the port-side freight doors have been removed to facilitate the Bird Man's exit.

I glance at Valentin. He is sitting hunched like a broody bird on the back seat. The wind ruffles his hair, combed straight back over his balding head. It stands up like the crest of a bird. He seems nervous—ill at ease. He crouches on the very edge of the seat. Sucks his lips. Keeps looking out of the window. Oddly enough, he confesses that he hates heights. An ascent of the Eiffel Tower once made him sick.

4-06. We top 9,000 feet and then drop to 8,500, the height from which the jump is to be made.

"Five minutes from now" says the pilot.

Valentin rises to his feet. Struggles into his parachutes. He fixes his main parachute to his back.

"Four minutes."

He straps another to his chest. That is his emergency 'chute. On top of it is a wooden panel carrying a stop-watch and an altimeter.

"Three minutes."

Tension increases in the plane. I find myself noticing little things. The bright blue wool jumper he wears under his olive-green flying-suit, the brown lamb's-wool-lined, suède boots with zip-fasteners and crêpe soles to take the shock on landing, the large gold ring on the little finger of his left hand. I notice, too, his watch. I am to see it again on his wrist. He will be dead, but that watch will still be going.

"Two minutes."

He puts on his goggles and crash helmet and a pair of red rubber gloves, rough-surfaced like those used by a gardener or wicket-keeper.

With his hands he indicates that his heart is fluttering.

He crouches down in front of the wings and starts to adjust the straps.

"One minute."

Valentin is nowhere near ready.

4-11. "Now!"

"Non. Non. Non!" says Valentin.

We begin a second circuit.

"Five minutes from now," says the pilot.

The Bird Man steps into his wings. He is facing the back of the aircraft.

"Four minutes."

He gazes wistfully out of the open hatch. The ground below looks like an unreal map.

"Three minutes."

"Is the plane with the photographers alongside?" asks Valentin.

"Two minutes."

Squatting on his heels, he edges, infinitely slowly, forward to the hatch.

"One minute."

4-16. We reach the jumping point for the second time.

"Now!"

Valentin leans outwards.

"Non. Non. Non!" he almost screams. "À gauche À gauche. À gauche. La rivière à gauche." He wants the Mersey on the left.

I find this hesitation strange. It seems to me almost as if Valentin has a premonition. I *know* he does not want to jump. Maybe some little voice deep inside him whispers that below is death through a mist of cloud.

For the third time we start that circuit.

Again Valentin asks: "The other plane, is it alongside?"

"Five minutes from now," says the pilot.

Once more Valentin begins to edge towards the hatch. He fights the roaring blustering gales that plucks at his clumsy wings.

"Four minutes."

Inch by inch, he advances.

"Three minutes."

His wing-tips keep catching in the ridging of the metal floor.

"Two minutes."

There can be no mistaking the strain he is undergoing. He shuffles doggedly forward into the main aperture.

"One minute."

I go over to Valentin, pat him on the shoulder and say "Bonne chance."

He pulls a wry face, gives the thumbs up signal and replies, "Merci, monsieur."

4-21. "Now!"

What happens now happens so quickly that it is difficult to be sure of it.

Valentin steps backwards and sideways to the brink of the exit, his closed wings held straight in front of him, his body bent, leaning backwards and half supported by the outside pressure. He looks rapidly up, once, . . . down, twice, and then it seems to me a buffet of wind catches him and whips him out of the aircraft into the slip-stream. At the same time I hear a terrible splintering noise above the roar of the engines. I see a tiny fragment of orange wood whisked away by the wind. Another piece hits the fuselage and goes spiralling like an autumn leaf to earth. The Bird Man has clipped his left wing on the side of the exit hatch.

46

A second, less than a second, later there is another crack, and the plane, which has been flying so smoothly that you could have balanced a threepenny bit in it, gives a slight rock. For a moment I am afraid our tailplane may have been fatally damaged. All is well, however, but Valentin is in serious trouble.

Leaning out, I am almost caught in the slipstream myself, but I catch a glimpse of him. He is spinning, clock-wise, towards the earth like a top—rolling, spiralling, madly pirouetting to certain death—his smashed orange wings glistening in the sunlight.

He has two chances—two parachutes.

We bank off to the left.

Anxiously circle above his tumbling body.

Watch helplessly.

He has fallen, I should judge, about 1,000 feet, when I see a little puff of white.

His parachute is opening.

But no. Instead of mushrooming out it remains cylindrical like a candle—a Roman candle—the stuck silk rippling like a flame.

Chance number one is lost.

Down ... down ... down, although he is plummeting at 120 m.p.h. the fall seems interminable. Time is eternity up here. To Valentin it must seem a lifetime.

What about the second parachute on his chest?

Heart-in-mouth, I strain to see.

He is about 1,000 feet from the ground.

IT OPENS.

It fails to develop.

God! *that* has candled too. It lashes around his face and wraps itself about his body like a shroud. I see him frantically struggling to free himself . . .

The long agony is almost over now.

The plane dives steeply in the wake of Valentin to within a few score feet of the ground.

And there below me in a green-and-yellow cornfield, spread-eagled, I see the figure of a bird—a bird with splayed and broken wings. He lies on his face, absolutely still, the only movement a slight ruffling of the white silk that looks from this height for all the world like the snowy pinions of a swan.

L'Homme-Oiseau a perdu ses ailes.

★　★　★　★

In his autobiography, *Bird Man*,* Léo Valentin wrote: "While I am

47

falling the idea of death never enters my head . . . Death is for the others, not for you," and he would often say: "I always get the firm conviction before I do anything that I am going to come out alive."

And had not his optimism been justified?

After all, it was eighteen years since he first discovered "that dark mistress, fear" in the sky above Baraki.

"The laws of gravity are inescapable and ruthlessly punish anyone who is ignorant of them or tries to flout them." But had he not dived more than 600 times into the spacious jaws of death? And was he not still alive?

Now, as he landed at Dover on this sunny Friday—May 18th, 1956—and drove his 12 h.p. Peugeot car up through the lovely, blossom-washed English countryside to Liverpool, he thought how lucky he had been. He remembered all those others who had 'made a dent in the ground'—young Raoul Sabé, his army comrade whom he had seen plunge to his death on October 13th, 1938, just two days before he had to make his own first drop; Clem Sohn, that *other* bird man, Salvator Canarrozzo, and that sweet girl, Baby Monetti.

It was a warm day, but he shuddered.

"I am nearly forty," he told himself. "It is well that this madness should stop. You cannot continue to stretch the limits of what is possible without provoking death—and that slut is not very loving if you flout her or pretend to ignore her."

Yes, this would definitely be his last jump.

He would receive £200 for it. That was the sum he needed to complete the deposit on the little provincial cinema which he was going to buy to support him in his retirement.

This time nothing must go wrong.

He booked a single room at the Airport Hotel at Speke. He asked for room 123—that would be lucky because it was the signal he counted before bailing out.

Valentin spent the next couple of days in preparation.

His wings were kept in a locked room at the airport. He guarded them closely and allowed no one but himself to touch them.

*Published in English translation by Messrs. Hutchinson in 1955.

The Dakota from which he was to make his jump had been hired from the Liverpool air charter company, Starways Ltd., and flown specially from the south of France for the occasion.

On the Sunday Valentin inspected it and expressed himself dissatisfied with the door from which he was to make his exit. He thought it too narrow. "If I have to jump through the ordinary door," he said, "the slipstream

will catch my wings before I am properly out and wedge me in the door."
He insisted that the freight doors would have to be removed.
This meant getting Ministry permission.

It was granted and, after ordering that both sides of the emergency hatch should be padded for fear he damaged his wings on them, Valentin signed a declaration certifying his satisfaction with the aircraft.

Just what it was that went wrong the next day we shall never know. Looking down at his rapidly-receding figure, I could not begin to guess. Looking up, a hundred thousand people far below were none the wiser.

They saw the silver Dakota circle the airport twice before a tiny object appeared, dropping like a stone.

They waited for the start of the bird-like flight.

Nothing happened.

They listened for the commentary.

The loud-speakers were silent.

An observer on the ground, watching through powerful binoculars, said afterwards: "I saw the Bird Man leave the plane quite clearly. He seemed to jump awkwardly at first, but levelled out and everything seemed all right. There was no suggestion of a glide, however, and when he had fallen 1,000 feet I saw a canopy and lines streaming out from him. Then his parachute candled and I could make him out frantically struggling to release his harness and level up. A little later I saw a billow of white silk. It was his second parachute. Then he disappeared behind a hangar and I knew that it had opened too late. The Bird Man had done his last act."

Another man, who saw Valentin hurtle over the rooftops of a housing estate and across a lane and railway line, lived on the edge of the field at Yew Tree Farm, Higher Road, Halewood, into which he crashed. He told me: "As I saw him plunging towards the ground at a terrific speed I heard a noise like the crying of a flock of seagulls—it was the Bird Man screaming."

As soon as we in the plane saw that Valentin was in trouble, the pilot radioed for help to Speke. The message was relayed by airport control to Lieutenant-Commander L. Tivy, a Fleet Air Arm pilot who had been patrolling the Mersey in a helicopter in case Valentin dropped into the river. We transmitted the fallen Bird Man's exact position and saw the helicopter speeding like a grey gnat to the rescue.

Meanwhile the first to reach Valentin was a Mr. George D. Hoyland of Formby. He had been driving along Higher Road when he first caught sight of Valentin. "He was at about 1,500 feet and I could see he was in trouble. His parachute didn't open and he went into a dizzy spin, crashing to the ground. I got out of the car and ran across the field to him."

The naval helicopter arrived. Landed. Then it rose again to chase an ambulance which was heading in the wrong direction.

A doctor came on the scene. He had covered two miles from the airfield in record time. Strangely enough, although I did not know it at the time, it was my own doctor—Dr. Mesrovb Barseghian.

Police-Constable Sevill of the Lancashire County Police, also summoned by radio to the spot, removed the parachute from Valentin's back to facilitate medical examination.

Dr. Barseghian bent over him.

He made a quick examination.

Severe head injuries. Broken legs.

There would have been no pain.

Death was instantaneous.

They covered him with his parachute—it was his shroud.

At midday on Friday, May 25th, 1956, just one week to the day after he had landed so cheerfully at Dover, we sat in the pink and eau-de-nil coroner's court-room at Widnes Police Station to hold an inquest on Léo Valentin.

For nearly an hour a procession of those of us who had in one way or another shared his last hours filed into the box to tell Mr. Cornelius Bolton, the South-West Lancashire Coroner, what we knew.

Mr. Charles Forbes Sealey, a retired group-captain employed by the Soldiers, Sailors and Air Force Association (on whose behalf the Speke Air Display had been organised) gave evidence of identification.

Mr. James Murray Kent, traffic manager of Starways Ltd., who had acted as liaison officer in the Dakota, told of Valentin's last moments in the plane. He said that on landing he examined the aircraft but found no indication that the Bird Man had struck the wings or tailplane unit.

Mr. Edwin Robert James, an aircraft fitter employed by Starways Ltd., said that when, later, he unrolled the carpet in the plane he found a piece of orange-coloured balsa-wood, about six inches long, which he realised was part of the wings used by Valentin.

Captain George Leigh, pilot of the aircraft, testified that before the ascent he had had some conversation with Valentin. He had told him that he had war-time experience of dropping parachutists and offered to 'feather' the port engine if the Bird Man thought there was any risk of being sucked out, but Valentin replied, "No, it's not necesary." Captain Leigh said that he was flying at 105 knots (120 m.p.h.) when Valentin jumped, and added that at that speed the tailplane was well out of the way. "I am certain that he did not hit the tail. A man of Valentin's weight hitting the tailplane would certainly have knocked it off. Even a sea-gull striking the aircraft at that speed would have dented it. There would have been a considerable disturbance to the aircraft if Valentin had gone even within ten feet of the tail." He concluded by saying that he, too, had dropped from a Dakota, and was convinced that the fact that Valentin clipped his wings on his way out of the plane was purely incidental. In his opinion, the Bird Man had made a bad exit and that was what caused him to spin.

Two of Valentin's compatriots also gave evidence.

The first, Inspector Jean Albert Errard of the French police, said that he was a friend of Valentin's and happened to be in England on holiday from Paris when he read of his death in the newspapers. "I knew him very well when I served with him as a parachutist in the British Special Air Service from 1943 to the end of the war. He lived at Brunoy and has given many exhibitions of parachute jumping in France." He gave formal evidence of identification. Inspector Errard confided to me that it was his personal opinion that Valentin must have blacked out when he jumped. "He was too experienced a parachutist to make such a mistake," he said.

The second, Monsieur René Chancerel, Principal of the Biscarrosse State Parachute School, near Biarritz, said that he had made 190 jumps himself, four or five of them from Dakotas. He had examined the two parachutes after the fall and his expert testimony brought a little light into dark places. M. Chancerel explained that Valentin apparently caught the edge of his left wing on the corner of the hatchway. He immediately fell into a spin and pulled the rip-cord of the parachute on his back at about 6,900 feet. The spin was so rapid, however, that the rigging lines became completely entangled. Indeed, they were later seen to have become plaited into a single thick rope. He used his chest parachute too late, as evidenced by the fact that part of the cordage remained in the container. M. Chancerel agreed with Captain Leigh that the clipping of the wings as Valentin exited was a matter of little moment, and that the main cause of the accident was a bad exit that developed the spin.

Dr. Mesrovb Barseghian then went into the box. He said that he was on duty at a first-aid post at the airfield and went in response to a broadcast message to the spot where Valentin had fallen. The Bird Man had apparently landed on his knees. His face was smashed and bleeding and he was extensively cyanosed. There had been no post-mortem, but he had no hesitation in ascribing Valentin's death to multiple injuries of the head.

On the coroner's direction the jury retured a verdict of "Death by Misadventure."

"There is no doubt," said Mr. Bolton, "that Monsieur Valentin met his death as the result of an accident. There is no question of the aircraft not having flown in a proper way."

He then told a hushed court-room:

"This is a very sad case. This man, apparently very air-minded, a pioneer in his own sphere, lost his life like many pioneers in the world of aviation.

We are very sorry indeed that he lost his life in such an unfortunate manner."

It was a pity that there was no relative of Valentin's there to hear that tribute. He had been married once and had a 13-year-old daughter, but he and his wife had drifted apart. As it was, Monsieur A. Pierre, the French Vice-Consul in Liverpool, who was present, rose and thanked the court for its sympathy. He bowed. We trickled out into the sunlight. An aeroplane purred overhead.

★ ★ ★ ★

When I left the coroner's court I decided to say my last farewell to the gallant little Valentin.

His body was in the mortuary at Whiston Hospital while arrangements were being made for it to be flown back to France in a French military plane the following Tuesday.

Four days ago, at the time of the tragedy, there had seemed something almost grand about it. It was drama of the highest order. Grandiloquent phrases about the blood of Icarus and those who flew in his wake not having spattered the earth in vain sprang to one's mind. Now, seeing him lying so quietly there, the whole thing suddenly struck me as terribly pathetic— the little man who hated heights journeying alone, friendless, to a foreign country, speaking not a word of its language, to die among strangers, smashed to pieces on alien soil.

Thank God, death would, as Dr. Barseghian had said, have been instantaneous.

★ ★ ★ ★

Driving back to Liverpool I had to pass close to the spot where the Bird Man fell. I had only seen it from the air. On an impulse, I stopped the car, crossed into the field of corn. Yes, there they were, two dark impressions in the green earth—that was where his knees and chin had struck the ground. But what were all those little bunches of flowers? A farm labourer told me. They were tributes of lilac, blue irises and *muguets des bois* scattered to his memory by local children.

It was a heavenly day.

Larks sang.

I gazed up at the sky.

It was blue—like a baby's eyes.

How innocent it looked.

But then, why shouldn't it?

It was the earth that killed Léo Valentin for, as he himself once wrote: "The lost parachutist knows the face of death. It is the face of the earth."

52

14. LIVERPOOL'S DAILY BANG

Since first it awoke the echoes and scattered the pigeons of Merseyside on September 21st, 1867, the boom of the One-o'Clock Gun has become so much a part of the pattern of Liverpool life that we seldom seem to think of it. Only the stranger discovers anything odd in the sound of a sharp report followed by a street scene of elderly gentlemen pausing to draw forth their gold hunters, and young men shooting out their wrists in unison. And yet the average Merseysider is as vague regarding the history and workings of the time-gun as I myself proved when, the other day, a friend, briefly here from London, gave me pause with a salvo of questions concerning the daily bang to which my ears since childhood have grown accustomed.

★　★　★　★

The origin of the One-o'Clock Gun is closely tied up with the story of Liverpool as one of the great maritime centres of England. A century ago this city of ours was famed for the excellence of the ship's chronometers which were manufactured here. Now an essential part of the stock-in-trade of the manufacturers of such instruments is a very accurate means of measuring time, and it was the daily custom of the chronometer makers to repair at one o'clock to the old Liverpool Observatory at Waterloo Dock in order to check their timepieces. When, in 1867, the observatory was moved over the water to Bidston Hill, the chonometer makers were exceedingly disgruntled until John Hartnup, the then director of the observatory, had the bright idea of firing off a time-signal, by means of which they would still be able to get the correct time from him, at one o'clock each day. An ancient 34-pounder cannon, which had seen service in the Crimean and earlier wars, was secured and installed on Morpeth Pier Head. This gun, which was set off from Bidston Observatory by means of an electric connection, was at first fired with 7 lbs. of powder, but as it frequently shattered windows in Birkenhead and, incredibly, a number in Everton, the charge was subsequently reduced to 5 lbs.

The gun continued in daily use—Sundays, bank-holidays, Christmas Day and Good Friday excepted—right up to 1932, though it was nearly spiked in the October of that year when the Marine Committee of the Mersey Docks and Harbour Board, whose responsibility it is, recommended that the time-honoured signal should be abandoned. At that time the old gun had been condemned by the ordnance authorities and a reserve gun brought into use, but the Committee felt that now that constant radio time-signals had become the order of the day the expense of maintaining the gun—then about £100 a year—was not justified. The public, however, came down heavily on the side of the gun and the Committee withdrew its recommendation. The War Office intimated its willingness to supply a new gun at trifling cost and,

53

on April 26th, 1933, a 32-pounder of similar construction to the original one arrived from Woolwich Arsenal, and the old cannon was rusticated to grace a quiet lawn at Bidston Observatory.

This second gun continued in loud service right up to September 1st, 1939, when a six-and-a-half-year security silence was imposed on it for the duration of the Second World War. In October 1945, a proposal was put forward to resume the time-signal. A third gun, this time a Hotchkiss 6-pounder naval gun, was set up in Birkenhead, and on June 17th 1946, the old familiar bang reverberated once again across the waters of the Mersey.

★　★　★　★

At 12-29 one sunny morning I stood before an innocent-looking clock—rather like one of those grandfathers of a bygone age—in the central room of Bidston Observatory. Beside me was the young girl whose job it was that day to fire the One-o'Clock Gun. One minute before she had sent a careful time-check to Morpeth Dock, and now she was about to test the electric circuit which is completed when two slender wires are brought almost into contact within the head of the fuse to fire the gun. Watching the second-hand creep slowly up towards the sixtieth mark, it seemed strange to reflect that once in every twenty-four hours that almost soundless clock, which neither strikes nor very audibly ticks, makes such a noise in the world. At 12-30 precisely, down went the switch and the quivering needles on a nearby control panel told us that 3½ miles away in the water-front gun-house the trigger had clicked down. The dummy fire, the daily dress-rehearsal without music, had been successfully completed.

Landing-Stage Seaman Alf Harris was just filling the shell with its 15 oz. bag of powder as, after a beathless dash to Morpeth Pier, I scrambled up the steel ladder and edged my way carefully past the projecting grey muzzle of the One-o'Clock Gun into the little brick-built gun-house. At 12-50 he loaded the blank shell into the breach of the gun carefully opened all the windows of the hut—"It's rather restricted quarters for an explosion, you'd better keep your mouth open when she fires," he told me, By 12-59 the atmosphere was, so far as I was concerned anyway, decidedly tense. Seaman Harris pulled the switches to the observatory down. We all waited for the big-bang, praying that nothing would go wrong. Six times in eighty-nine years the gun has failed to fire. Once on July 20th 1915, she fired twice and, scandal, on July 11th, 1935, she fired 35 seconds late. Mr. Harris stood by with a small stick ready to depress the trigger-release should the automatic mechanism go wrong. At 1 o'clock exactly there was a terrific explosion, a blue flash. I felt a thwack of warm air on my legs, the place filled with the sudden stench of cordite. A puff of grey pigeons rose high into the air and through my singing ears I heard the sirens wail acknowledgement of our timely service.

15. THE MAGIC RING

The circus, they say, has no home, but once a year it brings its sawdust-and-spangle world to Liverpool. One summer Sunday afternoon our streets are suddenly filled with an exotic parade—capering clowns, gracefully-costumed young women, stilted giants, and elephants, grey as the cobbles, lumbering trunk-to-tail—a colourful panoply, with more than a dash of the mediaeval, all to brassy music, and cheered by wide-eyed children and parents in Sunday best as it passes incongruously through the tranquil Sabbath-world of Prince's Park's trim Victorian suburbs *en route* for Sefton Park. There, it pitches its big top, erects its sawdust ring and clusters its mobile village of smart caravans protectively about its corner of the great Review Field which, for close on a hundred years, has been the scene of fêtes, fairs, and frivolities. The circus has come to town.

The procession ended, the crowds dispersed to tea and television, the real work begins. All through the evening and far into the night gangs of strong brown men in greasy trousers and polo-necked jerseys—the behind-scene heroes of the travelling circus—sweat and strain to make everything ready for to-morrow's show. Like journalists, they are always working against the clock.

When Monday morning dawns the great tent will bloom like a proud white flower on the field, miles of electric wiring will have been disentangled, hundreds of lamps fitted snugly into their sockets and a mountain of seating for 6,000 spectators will have been ranged in ordered tiers about the sawdust stage.

The amount of organisation which lies behind the 'greatest show on earth' is simply staggering. Take the problem of food alone. It is headache enough to convince even the biggest hôtelier, catering for the most ravenous clientele, that his is a positive sinecure. The weekly menu for eight lions is 600 lbs. of horse-meat. Twelve polar bears need a sackful of bread each, 140 lbs. of rice and 112 lbs. of fish, which latter they share with the sea-lions. For the 200 animals in Billy Smart's circus, 10 tons of hay, 12 tons of straw, 35 cwt, of oats, 7 cwt. of bran and 56 lbs. of linseed must be forthcoming every seven days.

Nor is it any joke laying on 1,800 gallons of water per week—1,400 gallons of which find their way into the dark interiors of ten thirsty elephants, the remaining 400 gallons being shared by the horses, zebras and camels. And on top of all this, there are 100 of the circus's 260 men, women and children to be supplied with four meals a day in the canteen. The miracle is that everything goes as smoothly as it does.

★ ★ ★ ★

Standing in the artist's entrance on the first night of the show, it was brought home to me not only how ageless, but also how international the circus really is. All around, I heard the tongues of Europe being volubly spoken, though German, I was told, is the official language of the circus, and the orders are invariably given to the animals by their trainers in German.

Speaking to one of that dazzling troupe of trapeze artists, the Flying Croneras, whose aerial antics brought my heart perilously near my mouth on more than one occasion, we suddenly discovered that we had both been in the vicinity of Rome just about the same time in 1944. That we had been fighting on different sides didn't seem to matter. Next to him was a lovely young girl who was only 12 years old at the time that we were soldiering in Italy. She told me her name was Shirely Watson and that she came from Birmingham where she once worked as a telephone-switchboard operator. Now, she is the Fire Goddess in the sacrifice-by-fire spectacle at Chief Sitting-Bull's Red Indian encampment, but her ambition looks upwards towards the high wires and the trapezes.

In the person of Charles Illeneb I met . . . courage. He is only a little man, this Illeneb, but he is one of the most celebrated lion tamers in the world. Last year he was savaged by one of his lions, Ceasar—"I lay on the ground with two of the lions tearing my legs and stomach to pieces. I thought I was finished, but I managed to raise my head and shout an order in my fiercest voice. The lions knew they had done wrong and slunk off to their pedestals as my assistant, Walter Milde, entered the cage." After a three-hour operation and 127 stitches Illeneb made a wonderful recovery. And his courage? Every night he goes into the ring and puts Caesar through his paces just as if nothing had ever happened.

And so, for two and a half hours, I watched the pageant pass with the pomp of an eastern caravan within the magic circle. I smelt the strong sweet scent of the animals, and thrilled to the curl and crack of the scarlet-coated ring-master's whip. Handsome young men and lissome young women performed impossible feats. Coruscant flashes of colour, they flew through the air graceful as swallows. The cries from the tent top as they launched themselves into space echoed above the upturned heads of a vast crowd that held its breath. There was beauty in the rippling muscles of men and beasts, the shining flanks of horses, the soft sand-coloured coats of the camels. There was beauty in the precision of every disciplined movement. I thought how like the ballet the circus is. There were surprises, too, as when the hideous gorilla which chased a screaming comic round the arena doffed its head to reveal the smiling face of quite one of the prettiest blondes I have seen in years. The clowns came and went. They did all the things that tradition demands of them with water and crockery and periodic explosions. Perhaps the most disconcerting thing of all was the chimpanzees. In their little red trousers and vivid green-and-yellow jackets they looked so utterly human I found their performance vaguely sinister.

And when, finally, Davy ·Crockett entered, complete with fur hat, bucking bronco and barking pistol, and the band struck up the theme song of the wild frontier, there was a roar from the children that silenced the lions, and all at once thousands of voices began to sing in time with the band. "Eh, Mister," lisped a very tiny boy with a pistol in his hand, "is that *really* Davy Crockett?" I assured him that it was, and I found myself remembering another small boy once upon a time had believed every bit of it and gone home to ransack his mother's wardrobe for the circus that *he* was going to put on in the garden.

I have just been taking the waters at the Liverpool Spa. The flat, slightly iron-tinted taste of the ice-cold water is still on my tongue, and although, mercifully, I do not suffer from rheumatism, I understand that the spa water used to be regarded as "tending to the cure of rheumatic complaints."

Actually, the Spa is a chalybeate spring which flows from the rock at the base of the cliff-like wall which lines the eastern side of St. James's Cemetery. It first came into prominence in 1773 when James Worthington, a Liverpool surgeon, published a small tract recommending its use in cases of loss of appetite, nerve disorders, lowness of spirits, headaches "proceeding from crudities of the stomach," rickets and weak eyes. A little later in that same year, another Liverpool physician, Dr. Thomas Houlston, wrote a more ambitious pamphlet belauding the virtues of the mineral spring and subsequently made a communication on the subject to the Royal Society. Though never styled "holy," the spring continued in great esteem, principally for the cure of disease of the eye, for more than a century, and I have been told by an old inhabitant of Liverpool that he could remember the time when hundreds of people would come from all over Lancashire and wait in line with small bottles to take away some of the precious liquid. Latterly, however, the Liverpool Spa seems to have fallen into disrepute and there are very few visitors to the spot where, beneath the pious inscription:

> *Christian reader view in me,*
> *An emblem of true charity,*
> *Who freely what I have bestow,*
> *Though neither heard nor seen to flow,*
> *And I have full returns from Heaven,*
> *For every cup of water given.*

the mirifical spring still spills unceasingly into its own stone basin.

At the time of the spring's discovery, the site of St. James's Cemetery was a quarry which had for countless years supplied sandstone for building purposes. Many of Liverpool's ancient buildings, including the Town Hall, the old Corn Exchange, St. Thomas's, St. Paul's and St. John's churches, were constructed of stone hewn from it. By 1825 the quarry had become exhausted and the Corporation, to whom it belonged, had to find an answer to the awkward question of what to do with the extensive excavation which lay like a Brobdingnagian wound in the heart of the town. Too immense to be easily filled in, it was at first proposed to convert its ten neglected acres into a public garden. It was just about this time, however, that the Middlesex authorities, faced with a similar problem, decided to utilise a disused quarry at Kensal Green as a cemetery, and the Liverpool city fathers gave their approval to the formation of a company which undertook the conversion of the quarry to a burying-ground. So it was, in the February of 1825, that a new cemetery in connection with the Established Church, and named after St. James's Church, Toxteth Park, was commenced. The cemetery was consecrated in 1829 and the first interment took place to the accompaniment of one of the worst thunderstorms of the century on June 11th of that year. Since then there have been some 57,774 interments, the last of which was on July 10th 1936, and now the old burial-ground is full.

Standing in the midst of this vast stone forest of memory, the eye is bewildered by its crowded profusion of tombstones. A little exploration is rewarded, however, by the discovery of some extremely interesting graves. Here you will find for instance, a tablet commemorating Sarah Biffin who, though born in 1784 without either arms or hands, contrived to become one of the most noted artists of her day. She worked with a long-handled brush, one end of which was secured beneath a pin or loop on her right shoulder, and the other she manipulated with her mouth. Her work was patronised by four British Monarchs—George III, George IV, William IV and Queen Victoria—and such was her fame that she is even referred to by Charles Dickens in Chapter 37 of *Nicholas Nickleby* and Chapter 28 of *Martin Chuzzlewit*. In later life she fell into great poverty but, befriended by Richard Rathbone, she ended her days in comparative comfort. She died at Number 8 Duke Street on October 2nd, 1850. Here, too, is the tomb of William Lynn, landlord of the Waterloo Hotel at Aintree; the man who may be said to have initiated the Grand National when, in 1836, he persuaded his farmer neighbours to permit an annual Liverpool Steeplechase to be run over their land at Maghull. And all about you are the graves of sailors and master-mariners who, after lives spent on the tossing oceans of the world, have found a final harbour deep in the still heart of this peaceful corner of Sailor Town. Among them lies Captain John Oliver, veteran of the Battles of the Nile, Copenhagen, and Trafalgar, in which latter he served under Lord Nelson on H.M.S. *Victory*. He died in 1876 at the advanced age of 102. And here, too, rests Captain William Harrison, who commanded the *Great Eastern*— the Great Iron Ship.

Scarcely had the new cemetery opened its gates when, in September 1830, one of its most distinguished sleepers was laid to rest in this quiet dormitory of the dead. This man was the Right Honourable William Huskisson, M.P. for Liverpool, who had the dubious distinction of being killed by Stephenson's first engine—the *Rocket*. His tomb is that small, domed, circular temple which dominates the centre of the cemetery and is its grandest monument. He rests within beneath a fine marble statue of himself executed by John Gibson, R.A.

I could not help contrasting the lonely grandeur of Huskisson's magnificent mausoleum with the humble stone which, amidst a cluster of indistinguished graves, marks the spot where lies all that was mortal of Catherine Wilkinson. Of less exalted rank in life, Kitty Wilkinson is every bit as much a Liverpool immortal as William Huskisson, and while the mountain of laurel wreaths has long since withered and mouldered away from the politician's bleak, locked temple, I found on Kitty Wilkinson's grave a beer bottle from the narrow brown neck of which sprouted a gay little posy of wild flowers. It was a tribute which she would have loved. This Kitty Wilkinson was a remarkable woman but it is mainly on account of her work during the dreadful cholera epidemic of 1832 that she is remembered. Apart from fearlessly nursing the sick and dying, she threw open the tiny kitchen of her own home so that people could use her boiler to wash the infection from their disease-laden clothing. Ten years later, the first public establishment of baths and wash-houses in this country was opened in Upper Frederick Street and Kitty Wilkinson and her husband were put in charge of the place which had come into being as the direct result of an idea that had been born in their own kitchen.

Walking through the cemetery, one sees here and there a broken cross, an urn toppled from its pedestal, a gruesomely decapitated angel. This damage is not so much the result of the passage of the years as the work of teenage hooligans who scale the inadequate wire-fencing at night and amuse themselves by hurling stones at the monuments. But there are other and less violent changes. The lichen has crept over old tombstones and smoke has mellowed their pristine whiteness to a sort of charcoal grey. Weather has softened corners which, like sharp-angled sorrows, have grown less acute with time. The snows and rains of the years have blunted the deeply-incised anguish of epitaphs until they have become blurred as old memories. And yet the hand which has erased so much extolling of virtues has left clear a terrible indictment. Upon the tall headstone of Sydney Evans, wife of John Evans, solicitor of Carnarvon, who died, aged 71, on May Day, 1833, is engraved the sorry story of a mother's pain:

"By her express desire it is stated on her tomb that she was the affectionate mother of a son whose unparalleled wrongs and persecution in Carnarvon, Carnarvonshire, Liverpool, Lancashire, perpetrated, brought her old age oppressed with sorrow to the grave."

There it is, an accusing finger perpetually pointing from the coffin. It is as if the sorrowing mother would pursue her errant son beyond the death-bed. All those wrongs happened so very long ago, and yet their graven record cries out across the years like an unquiet voice from the grave.

And everywhere is evidenced a gentler neglect. The shining ivy twines about its sculpted image and nature has drawn a kindly green coverlet of tall grass over many little mounds. It is well, for this neglect has brought a wild beauty in its wake. Although it is a valley of the shadow of death, upon a sunny day St. James's Cemetery does not strike one in that way. It seems rather, a little oasis of fresh green life in the stony bosom of the hill, where bright butterflies flit about in the warm sunshine and birds sing lustily in the sanctuary which has been provided for them there. It is a place to equal the lovely cemetery at Constantinople with its Piranesi-like walls pierced by tiers of catacombs, its sloping ramps, down which great hearses of the past lumbered, drawn by gleaming horses with tossing black ostrich plumes, and the beautiful little mortuary chapel, a perfect miniature Greek temple, standing darkly upon its escarpment in wonderful contrast with the flushed face of the new cathedral. Today, its surface no longer broken by the sexton's spade, the old burying-ground lies tranquil. It is a haunt of ancient peace and on long summer evenings it is the chosen rendezvous of youth and age. The children play among the tombstones; the old men sit and smoke their pipes, and if they think of death in these placid surroundings it is as a friend who comes with the soft-scented dusk to soothe tired eyes and gently close them in a long, long sleep.

17. THE CHANGING FACE OF SAILOR TOWN

It might have been one of those magnificent new luxury hotels, only the atmosphere was somehow more friendly than in those places where mink and champagne set their seal of formality upon the evening. Soft lights and sweet music filled the vast ballroom where more than a hundred couples waltzed gracefully around.

So this was how the modern sailorman whiled away those all-too-swiftly passing nights of shore-leave in the ancient Port of Liverpool! Here, in Atlantic House, the glittering club and hostel which opened its doors to seamen in July 1947, I was seeing for myself the final expression of a 150-year-old determination to provide worthwhile surroundings in which the men of the Merchant Service might enjoy themselves ashore.

A sailor's life in the old sailing-ship days, when clouds of canvas billowed across the Mersey sky, was not an enviable one. Returning, after long months at sea, with a full money-belt, the shellback found plenty of fair-weather friends among the parasites who haunted the Liverpool waterfront, only too happy to help him enjoy the good time he had promised himself. The old chanties have embalmed memories of the bomb-razed waste that was once Liverpool's Piccadilly. Paradise Street they called it, and to the seafarer of those days it seemed well named, for in it's quarter-mile of grog shops and willing "Judies" he found a sailor's paradise. But it was a paradise that soon turned into a kind of hell. As long as there was something left in the kitty it was all right. Liquor was cheap enough. "Drunk for 1d.—a blind for 2d." promised notices in the grog shops and women like "Tich" Maguire, Harriet Lane, Jumping Jenny and the big one nicknamed "The Battleship" were always ready to be your "light o' love." But only let the money-belt grow light and your love would soon scuttle you. Pretending sympathy, she would tell you that a friend knew a matelot on such and such a ship (naming one which happened to be in port) who had said that that vessel dished up the best grub he had ever come across. And if you heeded her you would, as like as not, find yourself signed on a vessel that was a coffin-ship. Again, she might betray you to a crimp, one of those odious waterfront opportunists who drugged sailors' grog and transported the stupified men to ships which were trying to raise a crew.

Such was the state of affairs when, in 1820, a benevolent band of philanthropists and churchmen began to concern themselves with the shellback's welfare and founded the Liverpool Seaman's Friend Society. At first, this society was purely a mission and confined its interest to the spiritual care of the seafarer. It secured a former merchantman of 800 tons, renamed it the *Bethel Ship*, fitted it up as a chapel and moored it at the north end of the King's Dock. Subsequently, three further chapels were opened on land—the North Bethel in Bath Street, the South Bethel in Wellington Road, and the Fo'castle on Mariner's Parade—and a launch was acquired in which the padres visited ships at anchor. Seventy-eight years later, the Society received an endowment from a wealthy Liverpool merchant, Samuel Smith, and was able to erect the building in Paradise Street known as the Gordon Smith Institute. This Seaman's social and residential club, named after Smith's 18-year-old son, whose death it commemorates, has since become famous all over the world.

In 1826 the Government presented to Liverpool an old ship-of-the-line, H.M.S. *Tees,* which had seen action with Nelson and was once the berth of Captain Marryat, the far-famed author of *Mr. Midshipman Easy,* for use as a Mariners' Floating Church. After her conversion she was moored in the south-western corner of George's Dock (now the Pier Head) where she continued in service until 1872 when she sank at her moorings. It was in this floating church that the Mersey Mission to Seamen began its work. Today, the Mersey Mission controls four clubs and has its headquarters in Hanover Street. Here, on the first floor, is a quiet, cool room which has been made into a chapel. It is also something of a museum, in which the Superintendent-Chaplain, Canon G. W. Evans, has preserved many little fragments of history. On one wall of this restful place gleams the brass memorial tablet to Fell of 'Frisco, the Reverend James Fell, sometime chaplain of the Mersey Mission, the padre who carried a six-shooter in his hip pocket and who, alone and unaided, cleared the crimps from the San Francisco waterfront. Here, too, is the little Chapel of the Convoys where, before a painted altar-piece representing a convoy coming safely to port, there burns a perpetual Lamp of Remembrance for those who lost their lives in Western Approaches convoys.

In Canning Place, close by the premises of the Mersey Mission, there towers the smoke-blackened bulk of the old Sailor's Home presided over by Mr. V. G. Winfield. Raised in 1850, from the subscriptions of merchants and ship-owners, it has played a vital part in providing good, clean and inexpensive board and lodging for Liverpool seamen. Prior to its emergence as the first institution of its kind, the shellback had to find a berth ashore as best he could. In the streets and alleys of dockland there was no dearth of places where "Seamen's Lodging House" was painted boldly above a cracked and dirt-grimed fanlight and where, at an exorbitant charge, the sailor would be bedded and fed—after a fashion. Some, such as Paddy Doyle's, were justly celebrated. Legend tells of how this amusing Irishman used to keep a cow's horn in his backyard and how he would walk a sailor three times round it and afterwards tell any Master who enquired as to that seaman's experience that he had been thrice round the horn! The majority of the lodging-houses were, however, poor places, from some of which the

63

shellback was lucky to escape with his life, let alone his money-belt! In 1860 the interior of the Sailor's Home was entirely destroyed by fire, as a result, it was suspected, of a seaman's penchant for 'baccy in bed, but, rebuilt, it has continued with its good work for the past 95 years. Recently, a smart new foyer has been added, but the beautiful wrought-iron gates of the gateway that meant home to so many old seadogs have been taken away and now occupy an honoured place in the museum of Pooley's at Birmingham where they were originally made.

The Sailors' Home continues to be mainly a hostel although it can boast a bar and a fine billiard room. The need for such amenities is not, however, pressing for in nearby Lord Street stands the Ocean Club. Founded in 1942, this is a non-residential club which has made the entertainment of the seagoing man its main object. How well it has succeeded in this aim may be judged from its immense popularity.

It is perhaps significant that both of the newest seamen's clubs—the Ocean Club and Atlantic House—have been established at points well beyond the boundaries of the quarter which used to be known as Sailor Town. This is probably due to the difference which exists between the new type of merchant seaman and his predecessor. Nowadays a great many seagoers do not make of the sea a lifelong profession. There is a constant flux of 30,000 men in and out of the service every year, which, considering that the total strength of the Merchant Navy is 150,000 (of which 40,000 are Asiatics) is a very high figure. The factor responsible for the change seems to be the de-casualisation scheme of 1941. Before the Merchant Navy Pool came into being, anyone could go to sea on any ship he chose and at the end of a voyage could remain ashore as long as he wanted. This is no longer so. To run away to sea has become a romantic impossibility. The new bureaucracy delights in form-filling and courses for everyone, from cabin-boys and firemen to stewards and officers, before they can point a foot on deck. De-casualisation has led to de-centralisation.

Things have certainly changed since the days of the sailing-ship men, and nowhere, I think, is that more apparent than at Atlantic House on the slopes of Hardman Street a mile from Sailor Town. I watched the seamen and the hostesses who partnered them (all part of the Atlantic House service!) as they circled the dance floor, and then I went into the bar and drank a toast with Father O'Connor, the director of the club. "To the men of Sailor Town," he said. "Past and present," I added.